READY-TO-USE
ACTIVITIES AND MATERIALS ON
PLAINS
INDIANS

A Complete Sourcebook
for Teachers K-8

DANA NEWMANN

NATIVE AMERICANS RESOURCE LIBRARY

VOLUME 2

**THE CENTER FOR APPLIED
RESEARCH IN EDUCATION**
West Nyack, New York 10994

10 9 8 7 6 5 4 3 2 1

Production Editor: Zsuzsa Neff
Interior Design: Bill Ruoto

Library of Congress Cataloging-in-Publication Data

Newmann, Dana.
    Ready-to-use activities and materials on Plains Indians : a
complete sourcebook for teachers K-8 / Dana Newmann
        p. cm. — (Complete Native Americans resource library : v. 2)
    Includes bibliographical references.
    ISBN 0-87628-608-2 (alk. paper)
    1. Indians of North America—Great Plains—Study and teaching
(Elementary) 2. Indians of North America—Great Plains—Study and
teaching—Activity programs. I. Title. II. Series.
E76.6.N48 1995 vol. 2
[E78.G67]
978'.00497'00712 s—dc20
[978'.00497'00712]   95-22854
                                                                                          CIP

ISBN 0-87628-608-2

**The Center for Applied Research
in Education,** Professional Publishing
West Nyack, NY 10995
A Simon & Schuster Company

Printed in the United States of America

For Elise, who introduced me to the Cherokees—and to so much more!

ABOUT THE AUTHOR

A graduate of Mills College in Oakland, California, Dana Newmann has been an elementary teacher for more than 15 years. She has taught in California and New Mexico and for the U.S. Army Dependents Group in Hanau, Germany.

Mrs. Newmann has authored a variety of practical aids for teachers including *The New Teacher's Almanack* (The Center, 1980), *The Early Childhood Teacher's Almanack* (The Center, 1984), and *The Complete Teacher's Almanack* (The Center, 1991).

She presently lives in Santa Fe, New Mexico, where for the past six years she has worked for Project Crossroads, a nonprofit educational resource organization. Mrs. Newmann heads the elementary school program and conducts workshops for teachers throughout the state and the Southwest.

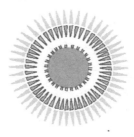

ABOUT THE REVIEWER

Eunice Larabee was born on the Cheyenne River Reservation in Lastry, South Dakota, one of seven children. Her father died when she was three. Eunice attended a United States Government boarding school and with the help of her grandparents, aunts, and mother she was able to get advanced schooling in Lawrence, Kansas. She worked for the Bureau of Indian Affairs (BIA) for many years and then became involved in tribal government. Today she enjoys the company of her many grandchildren and great-grandchildren.

ABOUT THE RESOURCE LIBRARY

The *Native Americans Resource Library* is a four-book series that introduces you and your students in grades K–8 to the lives of the peoples who have inhabited North America for thousands of years. The four books in this *Resource Library* are:

- *Ready-to-Use Activities and Materials on Desert Indians* (Unit 1).
- *Ready-to-Use Activities and Materials on Plains Indians* (Unit 2).
- *Ready-to-Use Activities and Materials on Coastal Indians* (Unit 3).
- *Ready-to-Use Activities and Materials on Woodland Indians* (Unit 4).

Each unit in the series is divided into the following sections:

- "Their History and Their Culture"—Here you will find information about the historical background of the particular region . . . food . . . clothing . . . shelter . . . tools . . . language . . . arts and crafts . . . children and play . . . religion and beliefs . . . trade . . . social groups and government . . . when the Europeans came . . . the native peoples today . . . historic Native Americans of the particular region.
- "Activities for the Classroom"—Dozens of meaningful activities are described to involve your students in creating and exploring with common classroom materials: native shelters, tools, jewelry, looms; also included are directions for making and playing traditional Native American games; foods of the particular region . . . and much more!
- "Ready-to-Use Reproducible Activities"—These are full-page worksheets and activity sheets that can be duplicated for your students as many times as needed. The reproducible activities reinforce in playful and engaging ways the information your students have learned about a particular region.
- "Teacher's Resource Guide"—You'll find lists of catalogs, activity guides, professional books, and children's books covering the specific region you are studying.

Throughout each book in the series are hundreds of line drawings to help illustrate the information. A specific feature of each book are the many historic black-and-white photographs that will help "bring to life" the Native American tribes as they were in the 19th and early 20th centuries!

The *Native Americans Resource Library* is designed to acquaint you and your students with this important and complex subject in a direct *and* entertaining way, encouraging understanding and respect for those people who are the first *Americans*.

A NOTE FROM THE AUTHOR ABOUT THIS BOOK

The descendants of the peoples who lived on this continent before the Europeans arrived have come to be known as Native Americans. This term is perhaps more accurate than Indians which can be confusing based as it was on Columbus's mistaken idea that he had arrived at islands off of India.

In this book you will look at the lives of Native Americans of the Plains and also Prairies: who they are, how they arrived here, and how they have organized their lives for the many centuries they have lived in this region. Then you will consider the effects of the arrival of the Europeans to the plains and prairies, and will look at contemporary Native American life in this region.

Occasionally present-day Native American life is cited in the prehistory sections. This is because in organizing this material, it became clear that in some areas, such as Language, Arts and Crafts, and Religion there are overlaps between the life and activities of the Plains and Prairie tribes historically and the way some of them live today. This emphasizes the continuity of attitudes and thought that has existed for them over the centuries.

Today it is essential that students realize their way of life is not solely the creation of 20th-century people. Much of what we eat and use, and much that is beautiful, has been given to us by the first inhabitants of this land. Our children should understand this, so this book will show you and your students the specific gifts we have received from Native Americans.

The Plains and Prairie Native American culture is based on each person having respect for all living things; it emphasizes what it means to live in harmony with one's surroundings. These are two essential lessons for each of us to teach—and to learn—as we enter the 21st century.

Anthropologists differ in their emphasis as to which tribes are specifically to be considered as Plains Indian. Because this book is addressed to teachers of young children, I have tried to keep information—such as Plains tribal groups—as simple and direct as possible. Some of the tribes on the far edges of the Great Plains wandered in and out of this area over the years and shared some of the ways of the Central Plains people; the Assiniboin to the north, the Nez Perce to the northwest, the Shoshoni and Ute to the west, the Caddo and Quapaw to the southeast, and the Illinois, Ojibway and Chippewa to the east are tribes that are often studied together with the Plains people. The Cherokees of Oklahoma were originally members of an East Coast tribe that was forced to relocate by the U.S. government.

The Sioux (or Dakota, Nakota, or Lakota) nation, which is central in any study of Plains culture, includes many sub-groups: The Santee, Teton, Yanktonai, and Yankton. The Sisseton is a sub-group of the Santee and the Oglala is a sub-group of the Teton. All are Sioux tribes.

The Blood and Piegan are sub-groups of the Blackfeet.

Here is a simple guide to the pronunciation of the names of Plains and Prairies tribal groups:

Apache	uh-PACH-ee	*Mandan*	MAN-dan
Arapaho	uh-RAP- uho	*Missouri*	Mis-UR-ee
Arikara	uh-REE-kuh-ruh	*Nez Perce*	NEZ-PURZ**
Assiniboin	uh-SIN-uh-boin	*Oglala*	oh-GLAH-la
Atakapan	uh-TAK-uh-pan	*Omaha*	OH-ma-ha
Blackfeet	(NOT Blackfoot)*	*Osage*	OH-sayj
Caddo	KAY-doh	*Oto*	OH-TOH
Cheyenne	shy-EN	*Pawnee*	paw-NEE
Comanche	koh-MAN-chee	*Piegan*	PEE-gun
Crow	CROH	*Ponca*	PON-kuh
Dakota	duh-KOH-tah	*Quapaw*	KWAH-pah
Gros Ventre	groh-VON-trah	*Santee*	san-TEE
Hasinai	hah-SIN-ay	*Shoshoni*	sho-SHO-nee
Hidatsa	hee-DOT-saw	*Sioux*	SOO
Iowa	I-oh-uh	*Sisseton*	sis-SEE-ton
Kansa	CAN-suh	*Teton*	TEE-ton
Kiowa	KY-oh-wuh	*Ute*	YOOT
Kitchai	KIT-chay	*Wichita*	WICH-i-tah
Kootenai	KOOT-nay	*Yankton*	YANG-ton

*Black<u>foot</u> is the name of a Canadian tribe.

**The name refers in French to piercing the nose, a practice of several western tribes, but not this one.

Today in this central area of the United States there are forty reservations and Historic Indian Areas, as they are called in Oklahoma. Each is specific to a certain group or groups, and the names are legendary—Blackfeet, Cheyenne, Pawnee, Osage, Crow, Kansa, Kiowa, the various Sioux, Shoshoni, Arapaho, Mandan, Hidatsa, Omaha, Iowa, Ponca—each distinct in certain ways from all the others. It has been my intent to write clearly and simply about a very rich and complex period so that even young children can understand it. For this reason, these pages offer only a first glimpse into a vastly fertile and unique culture. It is my hope that this book will be just the beginning for you and your students in your explorations into Native American studies—together!

Dana Newmann

CONTENTS

THE PLAINS INDIANS TODAY 118

HISTORIC NATIVE AMERICANS OF THE PLAINS AND PRAIRIES 124

THE PLAINS INDIANS: ACTIVITIES FOR THE CLASSROOM 131

THE PLAINS INDIANS: READY-TO-USE REPRODUCIBLE ACTIVITIES 157

THE PLAINS INDIANS: TEACHER'S RESOURCE GUIDE 195

THE PLAINS INDIANS

Their History and Their Culture

PREHISTORY OF THE PLAINS AND PRAIRIES

Between a million and half a million years ago there were at least four times when large areas of the Earth were covered with ice.

Sometime toward the end of the last glaciers—some 25,000 years ago—Mongolian people began to move across the Bering Strait, which was then a land bridge. They walked the 55 miles from Siberia to Alaska—and became the very first North Americans![1]

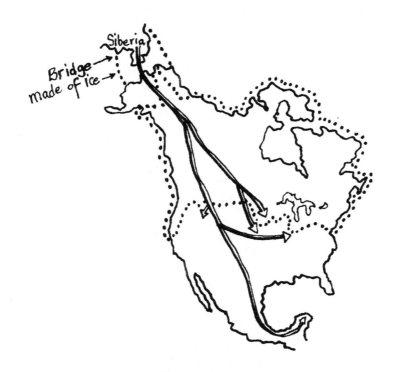

Over the next centuries the descendants of these people would continue moving southward until they populated the continents of both North America and South America—all the way from Alaska to Tierra del Fuego.

When we speak of the Plains and Prairies regions we mean roughly the area of the United States to the east of the Rocky Mountain range and to the west of the Mississippi River. Included are the present-day states of North Dakota, South Dakota, Montana, Nebraska, Wyoming, Kansas, Oklahoma, and Iowa, as well as parts of Utah, Idaho, Missouri, Texas, Colorado, Arkansas and Minnesota.

The Great Plains

Much of this area was a treeless grassland; the eastern prairies with their twenty to forty inches of annual rainfall had tall grasses; the western high plains, which received ten to twenty inches of rain a year, supported the shorter grasses. It was an "ocean" of grassland and it is called the Great Plains. From the north the freezing Arctic air swept down in winter and plunged temperatures to 40 degrees below zero; in the summer hot air rushed up from the Gulf of Mexico. Occasionally these masses met and formed the ferocious tornadoes of the midwest.

There were occasional wooded areas: stands of willows and cottonwoods grew on the riverbanks in the many valleys. Some geographic features—the buttes of the Dakota Badlands, the Black Hills of Wyoming and South Dakota, and the Ozark Mountains in Missouri—offer variety in the prairies' flatness, but on the whole this region was made up of miles of grassland—perfect grazing fields for the American bison or buffalo.

*"I was born upon the prairies where the wind blew free
and there was nothing to break the light of the sun."*
—Ten Bears, Comanche

PREHISTORIC GREAT PLAINS PEOPLE

The first people to live on the Great Plains (c. 7500 B.C. to 4500 B.C.) were prehistoric hunters. They would work as a group to stampede bison herds over cliffs or into swamps. These people learned to preserve meat by drying it and mixing it with fat and berries; this mixture was then stored in containers made of hide or animal gut or bladder.

It is not known what became of the prehistoric Great Plains hunters. We do know that by the 13th century severe droughts had driven the early residents to other regions. A hundred years passed before people returned to the Plains.

Then, sometime around A.D. 1300, tribes began to drift onto the plains again—from all four directions. The Pawnees moved into Nebraska from East Texas. Next came the Wichitas. By 1400 the Mandans from the eastern prairies had settled in present-day North Dakota. The other tribes followed.[2]

The following list locates where some bands and tribes were living in the 1500's:

eastern-most Idaho	Nez-Perce
Montana	Crow, Blackfeet, Piegan, Gros Ventre, Kootenai, Sioux
North Dakota	Hidatsa, Mandan, Arikara, Gros Ventre, Arapaho, Sioux, Chippewa
western Minnesota	Santee Sioux, Assiniboin, Ojibway
Wyoming	Shoshoni, Cheyenne, Ute, Arapaho, Kiowa-Apache
South Dakota	Teton-Sioux, Dakota-Sioux, Ponca, Cheyenne, Rosebud
Nebraska	Oglala-Sioux, Omaha, Pawnee, Oto, Arapaho, Cheyenne
Iowa	Yankton-Sioux, Iowa
eastern Colorado	Ute, Arapaho, Cheyenne
Kansas	Wichita, Kansa, Arapaho, Pawnee, Kiowa-Apache

Missouri	Osage, Missouri, Sioux
western Oklahoma	Kiowa, Osage, Kiowa-Apache, Wichita, Caddo-Kitchai, Choctaw
Texas	Comanche, Wichita, Caddo-Hasinai-Kitchai, Atakapan, Pawnee
western Arkansas	Quapaw, Choctaw

Here is a map for all of the visual learners:

Not many of those colorful hard-riding warriors and hunters of buffalo that we have come to know as the Plains Indians could trace back their ancestry in the region for more than a few hundred years.

Why did they come? There are several possible reasons: their populations were increasing and therefore they needed more space and land from which to obtain food. Droughts in their current homelands may have driven them out. (Later, the pressure of arriving Europeans would force many eastern tribes to move westward to the Plains.)

Once they arrived on the Plains the majority of the returning groups built their lives around farming. By the late 16th century the Blackfeet in the north and the Comanches in the South were the only non-farming tribes on the Plains.

With time these farming groups became semi-settled. Then, in the 18th century, horses became available from the southwest; many tribes—including the Cheyennes and the various Sioux—became nomadic as they roamed the prairies to hunt the buffalo. As you will see in the following sections, this extraordinary animal was central to the lives of the Plains people!

The history of the Plains Indians is unique among Native Americans in that their Golden Age evolved long after the first Europeans arrived on the continent. For it was the introduction of the horse—brought by the European explorers—that made a new vital life on the Plains a possibility for the native peoples.

Note for "Prehistory of the Plains and Prairies"

1. This is the common understanding of anthropologists, but it is not accepted by some Native Americans.

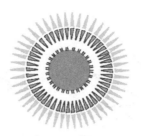

THE BUFFALO

The American bison, commonly called the buffalo, is the largest land mammal of North America. The name was given to the animals by French explorers who thought they looked like the French oxen, *les boeufs*, which the English and Americans heard as "buffle." This became "buffelo" and eventually . . . buffalo.

A grown bull stands six and a half feet at its massive shoulder, and weighs about two thousand pounds—as much as a compact car. The fur on its head and shoulders is permanent while the hair on its hindquarters is shed each year, beginning in March. New fur begins to grow in September and is at its most luxuriant by November and December.

Before the Europeans came to North America, huge numbers of bison roamed the Great Plains. There were single herds that numbered as many as four million. One of these could cover an area twenty-five miles wide by fifty miles long.

Not only was the buffalo the most important source of food for the Plains people, it also provided clothing, housing, tools, transportation (boats) and fuel.

Here is a guide to the many ways in which the buffalo was used by the Plains people. The sections that follow will explain them in more detail.

Meat	the most important food of the Great Plains people – also used as food for their pack dogs
marrow	eaten boiled or stored for later use in cooking
entrails	stuffed with meat, fat, marrow, wild onions and sage to make sausages
Hide	bull boat – drum – saddles – tipi curtain (to control draft) – saddle covers – shroud – horse blanket – Winter Count surface
calfskin	swaddling blanket for the newborn – game ball coverings – underwear – tobacco pouches
rawhide	hobbles – medicine cases – lashings for arrows, clubs, travois – parfleche – wristguard
winter hide (furry hide)	mittens – robes – coats – bedding
summer pelt	inner tipi covers
dressed	gloves – leggings – moccasins – dresses – breechcloths – shirts – cradleboards
neck pelt	rattle – shields
remnants	dolls

Hair	woven ropes – horse bridles – cradle board padding – stuffing for game balls – pillows – saddle pads
Horns	spoons – ladles – cups – bowls – tops – powder horns (later)
Tail	fly switches – switches used in the sweat lodges
Bone	fleshing tool – saddle horns – hoe
small	knives – awls – dice – arrowheads – scrapers – flutes – needles
ribs	sled
skull	ceremonial object
Stomach lining	stewpot hung on a tripod away from the fire, and later eaten
Tendons	thread
Fat	soap – ingredient in stews
Sinew	thread – bow string – beading
Bladder	jugs – containers
Hooves	religious rattles – glue
Heart	water bucket for warriors
Tongue	hairbrush (the rough side was used)
Dung	fuel

At birth a Plains Indian was covered with a calfskin swaddling blanket, and on death the body was wrapped in a buffalo robe. It is not surprising then that this animal played a big part in the people's spiritual life.

The buffalo symbolized power, long life, and abundance. Ceremonies were held in its honor and myths were told of its time on Earth. The very name of the animal had spiritual power. It was given to societies and to children in order to insure good fortune. Medicine men called upon the Spirit Buffalo for help in their rituals[1] and asked it to show them where healing plants could be found. A bison skull was used in the Sun Dance. (See **Religion**.)

Buffalo hunts were usually held in June, July, and August when the animals were fat, their fur was thin, and their meat was excellent. Autumn and early winter, when the animal's fur was at its thickest, were the best times to get pelts for buffalo robes. The winter hunting parties were small and the skins obtained then were used for tipis, moccasins, and bedding.

Before the coming of the horse, buffalo hunting methods remained very much the same for 9,000 years. If the bison were scattered, the hunters—each covered in a buffalo or wolf pelt—crept up on the grazing animals, shooting a few with their arrows without frightening the others. When the animals were in a herd, the hunters scared them from behind or set fire to the prairie in order to stampede them into box canyons, stone corrals, swamps, deep snow, or over steep cliffs. *Every* time these men went on a buffalo hunt, they were truly gambling their slender lives and bodies against enormous physical odds.

After the hunt the women's work began. (See **Food** and **Tools**.) Buffalo meat was dried and packed in containers for winter. There had to be large surplus supplies of meat for the group—the tiospaye—the extended families.

In 1800 there were an estimated sixty million buffalo on the Plains. But with the arrival of the horse, the rifle, and the European, the fate of the buffalo—and the life of the Plains people—were to change forever.

Strike our land with your great curved horns
In anger, toss the turf in the air.
Now strike our land
With your great curved horns.
We will hear the song
And our hearts will be strong . . .

—Traditional Chippewa song[2]

Notes for "The Buffalo"

1. One such ritual was the Teton Sioux Buffalo Ceremony that took place when a girl reached womanhood. In a sacred lodge an altar was built and on it was placed a buffalo skull and a container of smoldering sweetgrass and sage. The medicine man wafted the smoke in the four directions and also up and down. Next he prayed to Woman of the Buffalo God to help the girl to be a good wife, and a hard worker, to have a large family, and to offer hospitality to all visitors. After the rituals and various instructions, she was welcomed into womanhood and into her tribe as an adult.

2. As it appears on page 16 of *Turtle Island Alphabet* by Gerald Hausman (New York: St. Martin's Press, 1992).

FOOD

All people, in all cultures, have the same basic needs: food to nurture their bodies, and clothing and shelter to protect them from extreme heat, cold and rain. So it was with the early Native American also.

In the beginning the first Plains tribes lived in villages along the rivers or beside streams where the soil was fertile and easy to work. The land on the Plains was tough and hard to farm, so few early people lived there.

The women were the farmers and they had crops of squash, corn, beans (and tobacco).[1] The early Plains men hunted deer, rabbit, and elk. Hunting buffalo on foot was a difficult and dangerous thing to do; everybody had to help, so each summer the people of the village would go into the Plains on buffalo raids. Once an animal was killed they would pull its body back to camp using a travois: a platform fastened to two poles. (A dog could pull rather light loads on such a travois.)

MEAT

Buffalo

The meat from this animal (especially after the introduction of the horse) was the center of the Plains people's diets. Following a kill the tribesmen and women ate their fill of roasted meat and raw bits; the tongue and the hump were considered the "choice" cuts. Later, chunks of fresh meat might be boiled with vegetables and water.

The remaining meat was made into strips and dried on racks to become jerky. This in turn could be pounded into a powder and mixed with suet and dried mashed berries to make pemmican.[2] (See the recipes in **Activities**.)

Food was seldom wasted, for these early people understood that before long they might have to go hungry. Even the marrow inside the buffalo's bones was eaten.

Other Game

Deer, elk, prairie chickens, rabbits and small birds were other sources of meat. Some of the early Plains people caught fish for food, but the eating of fish was avoided by other tribes. Eating bear meat was also frequently forbidden for religious reasons.

WILD PLANTS

At first the people experimented with wild plants, learning to process those that had poisons in them. They milled, ground, and pounded native plants and seeds.

Sunflowers

Although these plants were found in the wild they were among the earliest farmed by Plains women, long before they knew how to grow corn, beans, or squash.

Turnip

This plant is called Indian bread-root, the prairie turnip, the prairie apple, *and* the prairie potato! Its roots were delicious as well as very nutritious and the Plains people harvested large quantities of them early each summer.

The large root would be peeled and enjoyed raw or it would be boiled, roasted, or dried on strings to be ground into flour.

Jerusalem Artichoke[3]

A native of the midwestern prairies, this plant is actually a sunflower. The tubers were cooked like potatoes.

Milkweed Pods

Among the Dakota peoples, young milkweed seed pods (while still tender and firm) were boiled with buffalo meat. They were said to make a tasty green vegetable, something like okra.

Berries

Wild currants, June berries, and gooseberries were picked and dried to later be added to pemmican or made into pudding. Tiny strawberries, blackberries and raspberries grew wild in the midwest also, as did chokecherries, buffalo berries, and wild grapes.

Nuts

Wild pecans grew in the Mississippi valley. (They were smaller and had thicker shells than those cultivated in the South today.)

Black walnuts and hickory nuts also grew wild and were prized by the early native people in the mid-prairie areas. These nuts were eaten as kernels or ground to extract their oil.

PLANTS GROWN BY THE PEOPLE

After a long while the Plains people began to raise certain plants themselves: sunflowers, beans, squash, and corn. Some anthropologists believe that the first domestication of plants may well have been for medicines or basket-making materials.

In the Hidatsa tribe of present-day North Dakota, every family traditionally had a marked portion of the river bottom land to farm; each lot covered about a 100-yard by 150-yard area. No one quarreled over the boundaries as "It was Indian rule to keep the garden grounds very sacred. We did not like to have disputes over them."[4]

Corn

Based on Buffalo Bird Woman's account of the raising of corn by Hidatsa farmers, here is a brief description of the yearly procedure.

Once the corn sprouted, the women hoed around each hillock to keep the weeds down and to retain the moisture. Scarecrows made from two sticks and old buffalo robes were used to keep off the birds.

Then in August, as the corn ripened, the women built a platform near the field. Here the girls, two to four at a time, would sit and sing to the corn, guarding it from horses, birds, or marauding young boys.

"We thought our corn liked to hear us sing,
just as children like to hear their mother sing to them."

Drying green corn for the winter was an extremely important part of food preparation. Here is how it was done:

1. Dark green ears of corn were plucked in the evening, just before sunset, and these ears were left out overnight in the open air.

2. The next morning before breakfast, the corn was husked and dropped into boiling water. When it was just half-cooked, the ears were lifted out with a horn spoon. Then they were laid on the drying stage to dry out overnight.

3. The following morning the corn was brought into the lodge and laid on a skin tent cover that was spread out on the ground. Using a small pointed stick, each woman ran this point down between two rows of kernels to loosen the grains; the right-hand row was shelled off with the right thumb and this process was repeated until the cob was completely exposed. The shelled kernels were dried on an old tent cover for four days. Chaff was winnowed out as the corn was poured into sacks for the winter.

Ripened corn was picked and husked during a ten-day period. The young men of a village husked the ears of corn that had been picked by each family and left beside the field. (In the 19th century young men were known to give particular attention to husking the corn that came from the harvests of very pretty young women!)

When long ears of good size and appearance were found, they were set aside for braiding. Usually 54 or 55 ears were braided together by their husks; probably this was the weight a woman could be expected to carry to a drying stage, where the braided corn was hung on the rails. The loose corn was laid out on the platform.

The Hidatsa and Mandan peoples took care of their corn fields during the whole growing season. The Osage, however, planted corn and then left it unattended while they went out on their summer buffalo hunts.

The Osage believed that corn was the gift of the Great Spirit, Wa-ki-do, and that corn had the power of giving life. For this reason, women and corn were closely connected: women were in charge of corn planting and corn rituals.

Corn was prepared for eating in many different ways. Fresh green corn was boiled or roasted on the cob; or shelled from the cob, put in a corn mortar, pounded, and then simmered without adding fat or meat. Prepared this way the corn had a sweet fresh smell and taste. At other times shelled green corn was boiled with beans and fats or spring salt or dried and used during the winter.

Beans

Six kinds of beans were commonly grown and eaten by the Hidatsa and Mandan; these included black beans, red beans, spotted beans, shield figured beans and white beans. Green (string) beans were eaten fresh from mid-summer until fall.

When cooked alone the beans were boiled with a piece of buffalo fat in a clay pot. Often they were cooked in combination with corn or squash or meat.

Squashes

Squash seeds were first sprouted and then planted.[5]

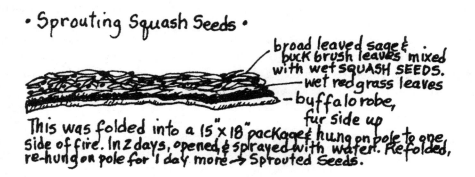

Once ripened the squash was picked every fourth morning before sunrise (and the fourth picking signaled that "the green corn" was ready to be harvested!). As squashes grow quickly, they must be picked every four days or they will become too hard to be good for eating.

Squashes not eaten fresh were sliced and dried. These thoroughly dried slices were stored in parfleche (par-flesh) bags (see **Tools**) to be taken to the winter camp, or were used when the men went on hunting trips. Any remaining squash slices were stored in an underground cache pit and covered with loose corn.

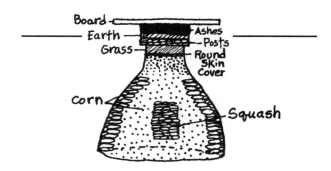

Squash Blossoms and Seeds

Squash blossoms and seeds were also important foods for these early people.

On a squash vine there are two kinds of blossoms; one kind becomes a squash and the other grows "at the wrong place among the leaves" and is barren; *this* is the blossom picked and dried by the Hidatsa and Mandan for eating.

The opened-out, flattened, dried blossoms were stored in round-bottomed calfskin bags with soft-skin mouths that could be tied shut.

Seeds were also dried and then stored in a buffalo calf bag (this bag was made from the whole skin of the calf, sides sewn together; the neck was left open to form the mouth of the bag). This sack was then stored in a cache pit along with extra corn and other dried vegetables.

Sunflowers

Seeds of the sunflower were roasted in a foot-tall clay pot right on the open coals and stirred to keep from scorching. Once the seeds opened up a bit and the kernels were dry and crisp, the pot was taken off the fire.

Then the parched seeds were pounded in a corn mortar to make sunflower meal. This meal was used in preparing Four-Vegetables-Mixed, a favorite Hidatsa dish (see the recipes in **Activities**) and the energy-giving Sunflower Seed Balls (see **Reproducibles**).

A common meal of the Hidatsa, Mandan, and Arikara was a succotash of pounded corn boiled with beans and, when possible, served with boiled jerky. Berries, wild turnips, and squash often supplemented this meal.

Notes for "Food"

[1]Many of the foods eaten in the world today were first grown by the native peoples of North America. Nearly one hundred plants—including many kinds of squash, nuts, beans, and berries—were given to us by the Prairie people.

[2]Pemmican is an eastern Algonquin or Cree word (*pimiy* means "fat" and *pemikkan* means "fat meat") that has come into common use in English. The Sioux word for this high protein food was *wasna*.

[3]Europeans carried these back to the Old World where Italians called the plant *girasole* (Italian for "turns with the sun") which sounded like "Jerusalem" to the English.

[4]We must thank a Hidatsa gardener, Buffalo Bird Woman, and her collaborator, Gilbert L. Wilson, for much of the information we have concerning the early Plains Indian farming techniques. In the first part of this century Wilson, an anthropologist, meticulously transcribed the gardening knowledge of Buffalo Bird Woman. Born in 1839, she grew to become an expert observer of village life in all its details. (See **Teacher's Resource Guide** for two fine books about/by this extraordinary woman.) I am very grateful to my friend Peter Nabokov for introducing me to these two books and to the poetic characters, Buffalo Bird Woman and her son, Edward Goodbird.

[5]To quote Buffalo Bird Woman: "We first sprouted the seed. I spread out a piece of tanned buffalo robe (18 inches by 30 inches) on the floor of the lodge, fur side up. I took wetted redgrass leaves and matted them into a thin layer on the fur. I put wetted squash seeds on (top) and worked in sage and buck leaves and folded (the robe) over and around it" making a 15-inch by 18-inch package that was hung on a drying pole to one side of the fire. After two days the bundle was opened and tepid water was blown or spat over the seeds. The bundle was re-closed for another day, after which the squash sprouts would be almost an inch tall and ready to plant!

CLOTHING

Before they had horses, early Plains people wore shirts, dresses, leggings, moccasins, and breechcloths made of deerskin. Their winter robes were made from furry buffalo hides or skin pelts.

The preparation of buffalo or elk hides was a group activity: many of the village women would work together to dress one hide. We can imagine that they talked and laughed together as they worked and that this made the task seem to go more quickly.

Plains Indians did not use tannic acid; for this reason it is most correct to say that they "dressed" their hides rather than "tanned" them. The method described below was used by nearly every Plains tribe. The only variations were in local ingredients used for the "braining mixture," the shape or materials of their tools, and the amount of time spent on each skin. The women always dressed the skins.

First, the wet skin was staked to the ground, hair side down. Any meat, fat, or blood that clung to the surface of the skin was scraped off using a fleshing tool (see **Tools**). Next, the skin was reversed and restaked so that the hair could be removed. The skin was scraped with an adz (see **Tools**) and each side of it was worked and reworked until the skin was of one thickness. At this point the skin had become "rawhide." If soft flexible leather was needed, the following further steps were taken.

A braining mixture—made of buffalo brains, fats, grease, cooked ground liver, meat broth, and a variety of plant products—was rubbed into the hide, which was allowed to dry; then it was soaked in warm water and wrapped into a tight bundle.

The braining mixture caused the hide to shrink, so it had to be restretched. This was done by alternately soaking it in warm water and pulling it down, using hands and feet, over a rounded post. If the hide was very large, it took two women working together to do this. When the hide was nearly back to its original size, the dressing of the skin was finished. The leather could be made even smoother and softer by rapidly pulling it back and forth through a small opening in a bone tool.

BELTS[1]

Belts held up leggings and breechcloths, and kept a woman's dress in place. They were especially important to Plains people as their clothing had no pockets: you could hang knives, awls, and pouches from your belt!

BREECHCLOTH

This article of clothing (also spelled breechclout) was worn by every Plains Indian man. It was a piece of soft buckskin, about 12 inches by 72 inches, that was worn by passing it up between the legs and tucking each end up under the belt. These ends, one in front and the other in back, hung down like small aprons and were often beautifully decorated.

When at home a man would often wear just moccasins and his breechcloth. Then as it grew colder, or when he left the village, he would put on a shirt, leggings and, if it were very cold, his robe. (See Photo 1.)

Photo 1. Unidentified man. *Courtesy Museum of New Mexico (neg. no. 152744).*

SHIRTS²

Early buckskin shirts were worn daily for protection and warmth. Each was made from two hides:

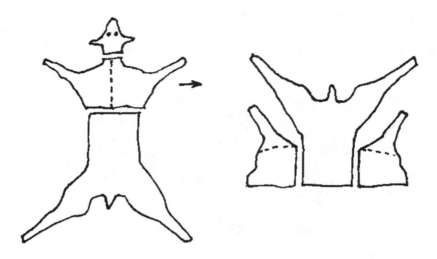

    The war shirt was worn only after a victory in battle and only by one in authority, such as a chief. War shirts were heavily fringed, quilled, or painted to record the heroic deeds of the owner. Blackfeet and Crow war shirts were often trimmed with white ermine skins. Dakota and Cheyenne war shirts used hanks of hair to show coups—acts of bravery.

Such shirts were considered to have great medicine or power and were thought to protect the wearer from harm. (For more details, see **War and Warriors**.)

THE BUCKSKIN DRESS

This was traditionally made of two deerskins; the dotted line in the illustration on page 24 shows the eventual shoulder line. The bottom of the dress was shaped according to the wearer's size and to the tribal style. The bottom sides of the two pieces were sewn together with an overhand stitch in sinew or leather strips. A running stitch was sewn along the dotted line. Next, the tops were folded down, front and back, to form the yoke. A neck opening was cut and hemmed. The sleeve sides were usually sewn shut or laced together.

Photo 2. Kiowa girl. *Photo by Carson Brothers. Courtesy Museum of New Mexico (neg. no. 144745).*

Fringe might be cut into the dress itself or sewn on, often along the side seam.

Early Plains dresses were worn long, down to the ankle. They could be decorated with cowry shells or quillwork.

LEGGINGS

These protective coverings were worn by both men and women and often their decorations matched those on the moccasins. The men's leggings reached from the ankle to the hip and the women's leggings covered the ankle to the knee. Early Plains men wore very tight leggings that were then split above the knees and tied around the thighs, or onto the breechcloth belt.

MOCCASINS

These lightweight foot-coverings are an example of how the Plains people combined usefulness and beauty in their handwork.[3] Often the front facing of the shoe was decorated with elaborate quillwork. Although their specific design varied from tribe to tribe, Plains moccasins were often made with a sole and upper of one piece of soft leather seamed at the instep and at the heel; they had the effect of muffling the wearer's footsteps whether on sand, leaves, or snow.

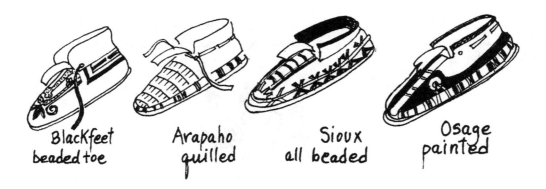

Blackfeet beaded toe · Arapaho quilled · Sioux all beaded · Osage painted

The specific footprint left by a moccasin could identify the tribe of the wearer. Sometimes, to fool an enemy, an Omaha might wear the moccasins of another tribe! This was not a usual practice because it was generally believed by the Plains people that to wear the moccasins of another tribe was to forsake one's own and to accept the laws of the tribe from which the shoes came.

"'Crees or men from across the mountain,' said Wolverine, examining the tracks. The footprints were wide, rounding; even the prints of their toes could be seen, because they wore soft-bottomed moccasins; all those of the Plains here wear hard parfleche soles."

—MY LIFE AS AN INDIAN, J.W. SCHULTZ, 1880

The Plains Indian moccasin made a firm flat-soled track; the Cheyenne's might have a small line behind it, as a brave of many honors could add the tail of some little animal to his shoe. The Kiowa/Arapaho added fringe to the back of their moccasins, which served to erase their very footprints!

Moccasins, being made of soft hide, would quickly become soggy in rainy weather, so an over-moccasin was worn for protection. These were soaked in oil and filled with buffalo fur to keep one's feet dry and warm.

BUFFALO ROBE

Ideally made from a two-year-old cow, these robes were worn with the hair inside or out, depending on the weather. The best buffalo robes were made from animals killed late in the year, when their furs were at their heaviest. Summer robes (of elk or buffalo) were hairless.

A robe might be elaborately decorated with a quillwork strip, approximately 12 inches by 48 inches, sewn down the center of the robe; four huge rosettes were often spaced along this strip and buckskin fringe would dangle from the center of each circle. Some robes were painted in one or two colors or displayed medicine designs or pictographs.

HEADGEAR

Sioux Winter Cap

Made of tanned hide, this cap fit close to the head and covered the neck and shoulders. It was tied under the chin to keep rain and snow from reaching the neck and throat. Feathers were added to the crown.

Fur Hats

The Omaha and Osage people wore brimless hats of fine fur, often the skin of an otter. These hats stood straight up from the brow and were ornamented along the top with quillwork and shells.

The Omaha warrior's hat was of this same style with the addition of a tail and a flap, both of which stuck out. Sometimes it was decorated with a quillwork rosette and trophy feathers.

Photo 3. Po-ne-no-pa-she, Osage Chief of the Big Hill Band; circa 1868. *Courtesy Museum of New Mexico (neg. no. 56161).*

Perhaps you've wondered how the Plains people kept their fur clothing free of fleas, lice, and moths. One very direct method was to lay a buffalo robe, for example, on an ant hill for a few days! To mothproof fur pelts, the women made a powder from the dried body of a martin or kingfisher bird and sprinkled this liberally over and between their fur robes.

(For other headgear, see Wars and Warriors.)

HAIR STYLES AND BODY PAINT

Each group had its own way of decorating its clothing and moccasins. Also, hair styles and body paint were clear signs of a particular tribe. Here is a personal description of the grooming of a Lakota woman.

The first thing a dutiful husband did in the morning, after breakfasting, was to arrange his wife's hair and to paint her face. The brush was the tail of the porcupine attached to a decorated handle. The husband parted his wife's hair, then carefully brushed and plaited it into two braids which were tied at the ends with strings of painted buckskin. These hair-strings were sometimes works of art, being wrapped with brightly colored porcupine quills and either tipped with tassels of porcupine quills or fluffs of eagle feathers. Bead hair-strings were later made, and they too, are very pretty. When the hair dressing was finished, the part in the hair was sometimes marked with a stripe of yellow paint. Next, the husband applied red paint to his wife's face, sometimes just to the cheeks, sometimes covering the entire face. If the woman was to be exposed to the wind and sun all day, she usually had her face covered with a protective coat of paint mixed with grease. It was "style" for the Lakota women to use much red paint, but the custom was very likely a necessary and comfortable one before it became a mere matter of style.[4] Many Lakota women had skins quite fine in texture and in childhood were light in color. Such skins, of course, burned easily in the hot wind and sun; consequently children were often painted with the red paint and grease, both boys and girls, the mother performing this duty and not the father.

—FROM LAND OF THE SPOTTED EAGLE BY CHIEF STANDING BEAR
BOSTON: HOUGHTON MIFFLIN CO., 1933

Paint was used by both men and women on their faces, hands, and the parts in their hair. Dried lichen from the Northern Plains provided yellow face paint; for black there was crushed charcoal or black pigment from the north. White clay came from the Missouri area and red clay was from the south.

Among the Hidatsa each color denoted the wearer's frame of mind: black was worn for celebrations (rejoicing over a dead enemy), red was for any joyful occasion (a dance or feast), light red and yellow were worn on a daily basis, and white showed that "you had nothing to rejoice over and you wanted the gods to come and comfort you."[5]

Notes for "Clothing"

1. A baby boy, when just a few days old, would have a soft belt tied around his middle "to prepare him for wearing his breechcloth."

2. "Among Blackfeet . . . it was not permitted for women to make men's clothing. Lone Walker himself cut and sewed skins and leggings, which he wore in place of those that wore out." (J.W. Schultz)

3. It was believed by the Plains people that moccasins should be made in such a way that whenever they touched the Earth she would see how her people were honoring her with the very beauty of their shoes.

4. Buffalo Bird Woman, a Hidatsa, recalled that she painted her face and hands every morning, so that her complexion would not get too dark. "In those good times everybody in the village appeared with faces handsomely painted. In these days we no longer follow this custom, and although living, we walk about with our unpainted faces looking just like ghosts." (Wilson, 1914)

5. Gilbert Wilson, 1909.

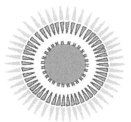

SHELTER

Those tribes that moved about a great deal had shelters that were portable: easy to put up[1] and, when it was time to move on, quickly taken down. The farming tribes, such as the Mandan, Arikara, and Hidatsa, built large permanent shelters. Some groups that farmed and hunted a bit would have solid earth lodges by their fields and tipis that they took on buffalo hunts.

GRASS HOUSES

This was probably the first style of house built in the Plains. Grass houses were low to the ground with pointed domes, covered by grass thatch. (See Photo 4.). They were built by the Wichita, Caddo, and Hasinai tribes in the southwestern Plains.

Photo 4. Unidentified Wichita village. *Courtesy Museum of New Mexico (neg. no. 4854).*

Seventy or eighty grass houses would make up a village, which was usually set in the middle of the fields of pumpkins, beans, corn, and squash the people farmed.

To build a grass house,[2] a ring of posts and beams was first constructed.

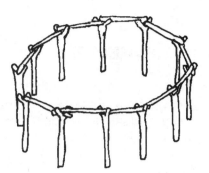

Next, poles were bent over this interior ring and were bound together at the top. This frame could be as wide as 60 feet across.

Sapling stringers, running horizontally, were used to strengthen the frame.

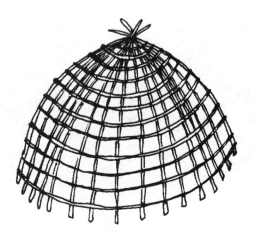

Finally, thatch was tied on in tight bunches. Outside rows of stringers held this thatch in place.

EARTH LODGES

In the early times there were many Plains Indian farming towns made up of earth lodges: big wood-framed, sod-covered houses. These were built along the Missouri and Republican rivers. They were made by tribes of "village Indians" who farmed the lands along the river (on the flood plains) and lived in these often log-walled towns from late February to late October.

In the Dakotas, the Mandan, Hidatsa, and Arikaras made their earth lodges beside streams that emptied into the Missouri River.

The Pawnee built earth lodges in the central Plains of Nebraska and Kansas, while the Omaha, Ponca, and Oto made theirs to the northeast.

All of these people put up their lodges in much the same way: four or more main posts—usually of cottonwood—were anchored in the ground and crossbeams were used to join these posts at the top, forming a square frame.

A larger ring of shorter posts and beams encircled this.

The roof rafters were supported on the outside ring and were laid out like the spokes of a wheel with the smoke-hole at the center.

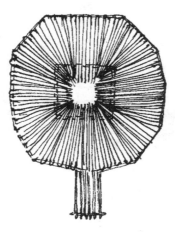

A side wall of split planks (puncheons) ran around the main structure to hold the earth walls. Small sticks covered with brush or grass made a thick padding for the final layer of dirt or heavy sod.

Photo 5. Pawnee Wind Lodge; circa 1868–70. *Photo by William H. Jackson. Courtesy Museum of New Mexico (neg. no. 58632).*

Some tribes then applied a coat of wet earth that dried to form a plaster-like shell.

Photo 6. Pawnee village; circa 1868–70. *Photo by William H. Jackson. Courtesy Museum of New Mexico (neg. no. 58633).*

An earth lodge might have three or four underground storage caches where food for the winter was kept. Each of these pits was six feet down in the earth, five feet across on its floor, and corncob-lined. (See "Squash" in the Food section.)

The Hidatsa Winter Twin Lodge

The Hidatsa built this unusual structure as a cold weather building. The main lodge was forty feet across and had a passageway that led to a smaller (fifteen feet wide) tipi-like lodge. This little structure might be made by a son for his parents or as a winter dining room for the family.

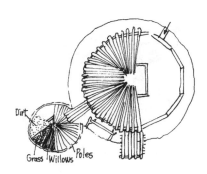

SACRED SHELTERS

In addition to special tipis built and decorated to hold religious objects or ceremonies, the most sacred shelter is the one built for the performance of the Sun Dance. (See Photo 7.)

Photo 7. Frame of a Piegan Sun Lodge; 1926. *Photo by Edward S. Curtis. Courtesy Museum of New Mexico (neg. no. 143859).*

Sun Dance Lodge

A Cheyenne myth, based on an ancient vision quest, tells how this sacred shelter should look and how it should be made.

The Cheyenne people were facing starvation because the buffalo had disappeared and so the tribe met and chose a man, Erect Horns, to go on a quest to help save them. A chief's wife went with him and they traveled many days until they came upon a hollow mountain. It had begun to rain and so they went inside the mountain and there, lit by the flashes of lightning, they saw that the inside of the mountain looked like a huge, extraordinary lodge. As they studied the lodge they understood how it was built and they were shown how to perform the Sun Dance ceremony. When Erect Horns and his friend returned home, they constructed a sacred lodge the way they had been shown and they did the Sun Dance with their people. And so the buffalo herds returned to the Cheyenne.

A Sun Dance lodge looked like a circular wooden fence about forty to fifty feet across. In the center was a forked cottonwood tree trunk freshly cut each year. Long radiating rafters reached from the circular fence up to the fork in the cottonwood trunk. The side walls and occasionally the rafters were covered with brush. Most of the Plains Indian tribes constructed these sacred shelters. (For a description of the Sun Dance Ceremony, see **Religion**.)

Sweat Houses

These sacred structures were used by the Plains people and continue to be used today to cleanse their bodies and minds. The sweat house itself was made of bent (willow) saplings tied together at the top or interwoven to stay in place; the Crow sweat house is made of 104 willows as was ordered in a powerful vision long ago. The bent saplings were covered with buffalo hides. Tobacco, tied in little bags, was often hung from the frame inside and a buffalo skull was placed by the sweat house or on its roof.

"At the entrance of the sweat lodge we dropped our robes or blankets, our only covering, and creeping in at the low doorway, sat around the interior in silence while the red-hot stones were passed in and dropped in a hole in the center. Lone Elk began to sprinkle them with a buffalo tail dipped in water and as the stifling hot steam enveloped us we started a song of supplication to the Sun, in which all joined. Then the medicine pipe was filled, lighted with a coal which was passed in, and as it was passed around, each one after blowing a whiff of smoke toward the heavens and the earth, made a short prayer to the Sun, to Old Man and Mother Earth."

—My Life as an Indian, J.W. Schultz, 1880

Each tribe had its own special prayers, songs, and symbols for use during a sweat. Those in the sweat house would lash themselves with sage branches or a buffalo tail to open the pores in their skin. After the sweat the people would usually go jump in an icy stream or river—even in winter. The sweat was followed by a feast.

THE TIPI[3]

The inner frame of the tipi was a cone of peeled poles of red cedar or lodge pole pine. This was covered with half a circle of twelve or more tanned buffalo hides that had been sewn together. The doorway of the tipi was usually made to face east. The flaps high up at the top of the cone were opened or closed to ward off the wind or to let out the smoke from the fire inside.

A tipi lining was tied onto the poles inside. Its decoration made the inside of the tipi more pleasant and colorful, but the main reasons for using this cloth were that it kept water from running down the tipi poles and it cut down on drafts; it also acted as an air passage to carry smoke up to the smoke flaps above.

Tipis were made in two ways. In the southern Plains a three-pole tipi base frame was common. Such tipis were used by the Kiowa, Arapaho, Kiowa-Apache, Pawnee, Omaha, Ponca, Cheyenne, Sioux, Nez Perce, Shoshoni, and Wichita.

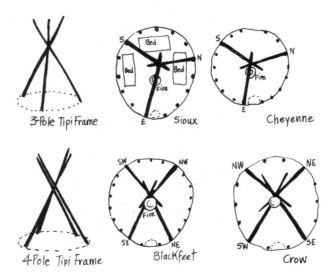

To the north a four-pole foundation, which gave a larger interior, was generally used. Additional poles (from seven to seventeen) were added to fill in around the main ones. Four-poled tipis were used by the Blackfeet, Crow, Hidatsa, Mandan, Arikara, Comanche, and some Nez Perce.

The floor of a tipi was rather egg-shaped. The side view looked like a tilted cone with the steeper side facing west, the direction from which most wind came. This shape also allowed the fire to be directly under the smoke flaps.

Photo 8. Blackfeet ceremonial. *Photo by H. F. Robinson. Courtesy Museum of New Mexico (neg. no. 26795).*

To construct the tipi, the cover was tied to the middle pole on the western side of the frame. Then it was pulled around both sides, meeting at the doorway. It was important to place the additional poles correctly so that the tipi cover would fit tightly at the front (where it was laced together using willow pins) and at the bottom (where it was pegged to the ground).

The smoke flaps could be opened and closed from inside by moving a pair of long poles. Each pole was placed in a pocket at the top of one of the flaps; the bottom of each flap was tied to a stake by the door. (See Photo 9.)

Photo 9. Shakaptian, Nez Perce lodges in the village. *Courtesy Museum of New Mexico (neg. no. 68267).*

There were fixed places in the tipi, ordered by social custom,[4] for seating, sleeping and the storage of personal and sacred objects; furnishings could include willow stick backrests, buffalo robes, rawhide trunks, and beds of tanned furs.

Photo 10. Blackfeet man sitting in tipi. *Courtesy Museum of New Mexico (neg. no. 26800).*

The door usually faced the rising sun. The oldest man slept at the back on the western side. Men sat on the northern side and women on the southern. If the tipi held more than one family or more than one wife, personal household objects would show where each slept. Medicine bundles were often hung on tripods inside the tipi, or attached high up on the tipi cover. Firewood, cooking utensils, and food were kept outside by the door.

That Wind

That wind, that wind,
Shakes my tipi, shakes my tipi,
And sings a song for me.
And sings a song for me.
　　—Kiowa

Notes for "Shelter"

1. It took about an hour for a woman to put up a tipi.

2. Traditionally, the culture hero Red Bean Man, messenger of the great spirit Kinnikasus, told the Wichita how to build a grass house:

" . . . in the future the homes for all the people will be as this house which the spirit told me how to build; for they are good, and in them the tribe will have good health. First, the women will make the ground ready: they will cut away the sod on the chosen space and make smooth the surface with the pure earth. In shape it will be round like the sun. The men will go to the forest and cut many short cedar posts with crotches at the top. Of these, four of the best will be planted in the ground, in the shape of a square, beginning at the east. All of these posts must be made fine and smooth, or the spirits will say our work is not good. When the four posts of the house are secured in position, then you will set up others about them that the form of the house may be round. In the crotches you will lay other fine cedar timbers, against which will lay all outer timbers. Next you will divide the workers into four parties, the leader of each taking his men to one point of the land; the first to the south, the next to the west, then one to the north and one to the east. Each party will cut and prepare a fine long cedar. These four from the four winds are the strength of the house. They are like the chiefs who hold up the tribe. Before these men and their leaders go out to look for the fine cedars, they will pray to Kinnikasus that their work may be good; that the cedars which they find may give the house great strength, and that through the strength of the house the people may prosper . . . "

Edward S. Curtis collected this Red Bean Man narrative in the 1920's. It appears in *Native American Architecture* by Peter Nabokov and Robert Easton (New York: Oxford University Press, 1990).

3. This is a Siouan word meaning "used to stay or live in." The oldest sign of Plains tribes' shelters are the "tipi rings": circles of rocks that are believed to have been used to hold down the bottoms of small hide-covered tents. Most often these rings are found on ridges. Perhaps they were placed there to keep snow from drifting and covering their little tents.

4. There were also special rules for behavior inside a tipi: Never go into a tipi without first having been invited. Once inside, go to the left if you are a female; move to the right if you are a male. Never walk between the fire and the elder(s) or other guests. Do not start a conversation with the elder, but wait for him to speak first. Bring your own bowl and spoon if dinner is to be served. Eat all the food you are served and, lastly, clean your pipe only when the host cleans his.

TOOLS

The Plains Indians constructed and used a variety of tools and utensils that made their lives easier and more efficient. These tools were a help in hunting, farming, and food preparation.

FOR FARMING

Digging Stick

Made of pine or ash, this tool had one end knobbed and the other carved to a point that became polished with use. The handle was about 35 inches long.

"A digging stick was a very important instrument; besides its use in the garden and for digging up turnips it was used for making tent-pin holes, post holes, or in fact for any kind of hole and it was used as a crowbar for rolling logs," Buffalo Bird Woman reported to Wilson in 1912.

Digging sticks also had sacred uses and were sometimes included in medicine bundles (see **Religion**).

Rake

Either made of wood or from the antler of a black-tailed deer, such a tool was used for clearing the edges of a field, or during the burning of trash in the spring.

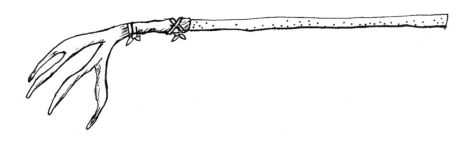

Hoe

This tool was made of an elm wood handle attached to a buffalo's shoulder blade. It was used by a woman to hoe her garden.

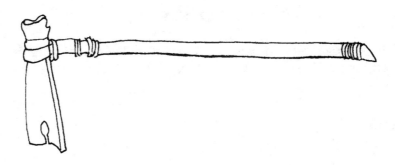

Burden Basket

Such a basket was used by a woman to carry corn, squash, and beans from the fields. One kind was made of dyed and undyed willow and elder bark woven in chevron and diamond patterns on a frame made of bent willows. A second type of burden basket was made of skin sewn over a willow frame.

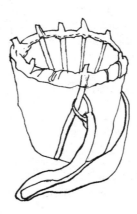

FOR HUNTING

Bow and Arrows

Because of its strength ash was the best wood for making bows. The Hidatsa shaved the upper arm of the bow to give it a greater bend when the string was drawn. This also helped steady and straighten the arrow's flight. By using different shapes and woods (ash, plum, cedar, elm, chokecherry) the bow maker gave it different qualities.

Photo 11. Lone Bear, Pawnee. *Photo by Harold Kellogg. Courtesy Museum of New Mexico (neg. no. 77515).*

The bowstring was made of twisted sinew. A rawhide wristguard was worn to protect the hunter's skin from the severe rebound of the bowstring.

There were many different kinds of arrows: blunt-headed for shooting birds and small rodents, wooden-pointed for boys hunting mice and rabbits. Crossbars near the point were used when shooting up into the trees, as such an arrow would fall to earth and stick upright in the ground, making it easier to find. Spiral fletching on an arrow had religious importance.

Arrowheads (projectile points) were carved from stone, obsidian or, sometimes, from flat pieces of bone. An obsidian or flint-pointed arrow drawn back on an average 60-pound bow could go through the body of a buffalo. (This means that to fully draw this bow, a force equal to lifting 60 pounds had to be applied.)

TOOLS AND UTENSILS FOR FOOD PREPARATION

Corn Mortar

These wooden mortars were used by the Mandans and the Hidatsas. The mortar was made from a hollow log and sunk into the lodge floor so a woman could sit as she pounded the dried corn, meat, or other food. The ash wood pestle was used with the large end up.

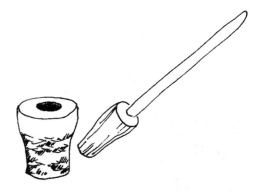

Stone Hammers

Such tools were used to pound berries, dried meat, and vegetables. The hammer had a stone head and a wooden handle, both wrapped in a rawhide sheath.

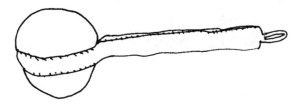

Squash Knife

This tool was made from the thin part of a buffalo cow's shoulder bone, which was thinner than that of a deer, bear, or elk. It was cut from a green bone, which is thin and hard, and will, therefore, keep an edge. It was used only for slicing squash and would last a very long time.

Spoons and Ladles

These had many uses, such as dipping out hot food from a pot on the coals. They were commonly made from buffalo horn, but other materials were also used. The Crow made them out of the horn of mountain sheep.

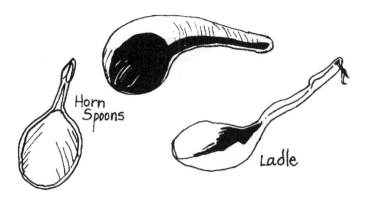

The Hidatsa split squash stems at one end and held the split open with a little stick; they handled fresh green corn and beans with the help of this "spoon."

Cooking Pots

Most of the nomadic Plains people preferred baskets or hide containers to clay ones, as they were less fragile. The Mandan and Hidatsa made vessels of fired brown clay tempered with crushed rock. Such pots when used for water were set on willow rings and never on the dirt as "Our clay pots were considered sacred." (Wolf Chief)

A buffalo paunch cooking vessel was held by four poles and stood to one side of the fire where a woman would drop hot stones into its contents, bringing the soup or stew to a boil. These pots would soften after a few days and would then be replaced.

CONTAINERS

Leather containers used to carry food and other items were made in many styles. The Crow, Cheyenne and Sioux used what they called a "possible bag"—because it was possible to store so many different things in it. The front of such a bag might be of various dressed leathers. It would be decorated with quillwork and, perhaps, feathers.

Parfleche

A *parfleche* was a rawhide bag used by many Plains groups, among them the Blackfeet, Crow, Nez Perce, Gros Ventre, and Hidatsa. (When French explorers saw rawhide shields being used to deflect arrows, they called the leather used in these shields *parfleche,* which means "it turns arrows aside.") This case was made from one piece of leather that was folded over and then sewn up with tanned hide strips. Women usually decorated these cases with geometric designs.

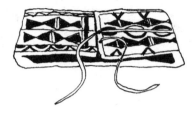

Bags might also be made from an unborn buffalo calf hide turned so that the hair was inside and with all but one opening sewn shut. Then the hide was inflated, softened by hand, and hung to dry. Once dry a flap was sewn along the opening and the bag was turned right side out once more.

WARRING TOOLS

The main weapons used by Plains warriors when they fought on foot were lances, clubs, bows, arrows, and shields.

Lance

This was a round ash shaft about six feet long with a blade inserted at one end and secured with sinew-sewn rawhide.

Bow and Arrow

Bows made for warfare were constructed of very heavy wood so that they could be used, if necessary, as clubs.

Quiver and Bow-case

Such holders were slung across the warrior's back as he went into battle and held his arrows and bows.

War Shields

The war shield was a brave's most prized possession. It protected him in battle and, in the end, it was laid under his head at his death.

Shield Cover   Arapaho   Blackfeet Shield

(For more information on shields, see **Arts and Crafts** and **War and Warriors**.)

Clubs

These weapons were made of bone, wood, and stone. They included ball and spike clubs, stone-headed clubs, bone clubs held to the wrist by a rawhide wristband, and slingshot clubs that were used to propel a heavy rock into the enemy's ranks.

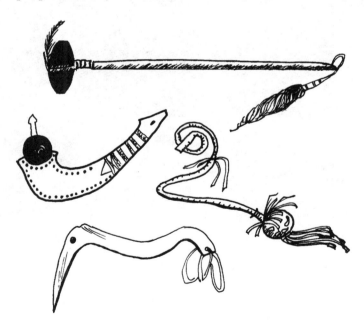

Heartskin Bucket

It was, as its name indicates, made from a buffalo's heart and was used by the young helpers to bring water to the men on the warpath.

Photo 12. Cheyenne Chief Minimic and his son Howling Wolf, prisoners of war, Fort Marion, Florida; circa 1871–75. *Courtesy Museum of New Mexico (neg. no. 70549).*

LANGUAGE

When Christopher Columbus arrived on the shores of the New World, there were three hundred languages being spoken among the people north of Mexico. These were separate languages, not dialects, as speakers of one language would not understand speakers of another. This shows how varied the North American Indian culture was before the Conquest.

These languages were divided into eight major linguistic groups. The languages of the Plains and Prairie peoples belong to the following families:

Linguistic group	Tribal languages from this group
Athabaskan	Lipan-Apache, Kiowa-Apache, Sarcee
Algonquian	Cheyenne, Sauk, Fox, Arapaho, Plains Ojibway, Plains Cree, Blackfeet, Piegan, Gros Ventre
Siouan	Lakota, Dakota and Nakota Sioux; Crow, Hidatsa, Mandan, Oto, Osage, Ponca, Kansa, Quapaw, Missouri
Caddoan	Kiowa
Shoshonean (Uto Aztec)	Ute, Shoshoni, Comanche

During the 18th and 19th centuries, languages of the *Algonquian* (Northern Plains) and *Siouan* (Central Plains) families dominated on the Great Plains, while *Athabaskan* and *Shoshonean* languages were used most often on the southern plains.

Here are some things you can say in the Dakota-Sioux language:

"Hoh-you kohdah."	"Hello, friend."
"Hoh-you kechyouwah."	"Hello, darling."
"Tokaytyou hay?"	"How are things?" "How're you doing?"
"Wah-stay."	"Good."
"Tnayou-wahyou-ahn."	"Very well."

"Kohwah'-keepay-snee."   "I'm afraid not so (well)."

"Wah younch chyoun."   "I'm sorry."

"Hleehay'-eeceeyHohah-poh!"   "Take courage. (Cheer up.)"

"Hee.Hee."   "Thanks."

"Heen-yahnkah poh."   "Hold on. Don't go."

"Tahn yahn."   "Everything's OK."

"Oh'-wahkeeyeen ktay."   "I'll help."

"Tah'kyou-yahkah'-payloh."   "I believe you."

"Njoun way!"   "So be it."

(See the activity pages for many more words in various Plains Indian languages.)

PLACE NAMES WE GET FROM THE PLAINS INDIANS

The Native Americans of the prairies and the Great Plains have given us a large number of words in common use in America. Many of our cities, including Wichita, Sioux City, Cheyenne, Iowa City, Kansas City and Oklahoma City, as well as bodies of water such as the Missouri and Mississippi rivers, have Native American names.

There are over a dozen central States with names derived from the native people:

Idaho is believed to come from "Edah hoe," a Shoshoni translation of the phrase "light on the mountains." (Another suggestion is that Idaho means "salmon eaters" from the Shoshoni "ida" [salmon] and "ho" [tribe, eaters].

Illinois comes from the Illini Indians who lived in this area originally; "Illiniwen," meaning "the men (warriors)," was supplemented with the French adjective ending "ois."

Iowa takes its name from the river named by the Ioway Indians. It has been said to mean "This is the place" as well as "beautiful place," "gray snow," and even "sleepy ones."

Kansas was named for the Kansa tribe of Siouan Indians who at first lived in that area. The name translates as "(south) wind people."

Minnesota is from the Dakota word meaning "sky-tinted water."

Mississippi means "great river" or "gathering of all the waters," and sometimes was referred to as "father of waters." It was at first recorded as "Michi Sepe."

Missouri is a native word meaning "muddy water."

Nebraska is an Omaha or Sioux word describing the river of this state and means "flat or broad river."

North Dakota and *South Dakota*: The Dakota peoples lived in the region where these states are located. Dakota means "allies" and referred to the Lakota, Nakota and Dakota as a group.

Oklahoma means "the Red People," and was first used in the Indian Territory by a Choctaw-speaking missionary in 1866.

Texas comes from the Caddo people's greeting, "Taysha," meaning "Friend."

Utah comes from an Apache word, "yuttahih," meaning "the ones who are higher up" and was applied to the Ute people who lived up in the mountains above the Apaches.

Wyoming was first used to refer to the Wyoming Valley of Pennsylvania; it comes from a Delaware Indian word, "maugh-wau-wama," meaning "upon the great plains."

POETIC EXPRESSION

It has been said that the early Native Americans thought in terms of images or mental pictures and frequently spoke in symbols. Their lives were closely linked to nature and its cycles and very often their speech reflected this. A good example of this are the names they gave to "the months" or times of seasonal shifts.

The Names of "The Months" [1]

JANUARY

The Omaha Indians of Nebraska call January "When the Snow Drifts into the Tents of the Honga." The Dakota call this "Hard Moon." To the Iowa tribes it is "Raccoon Month" and the Pawnee call this season Puhuwat—"The Entrance to the Earth Lodge."

FEBRUARY

The Omaha people call February "The Moon When Geese Come Home." If the Pawnee heard thunder from the north, they took it as a sign that cold weather would last into spring and named this month "Thunder" or "Snow-it-is-White."

MARCH

The Crow Indians call this month "When the Ice Breaks" and the Pawnee call it "Clearing." To the Dakota it is "Sore Eye Moon" and the Omahas refer to it as "Little Frog Moon."

APRIL

To the Dakota this month is "Moon in Which the Geese Lay Eggs" and the Omaha people say this is the "Moon in Which Nothing Happens." The Crow month called "When the Leaves Sprout" falls between April and May. The Pawnee call this "Planting Time."

MAY

Both the Omahas and the Dakotas call this month "Planting Moon."

JUNE

The Pawnees recognized a time in mid-June that they referred to as "Standing Alone" because this was when tribal members went off on their summer hunt. The Dakotas call this season "Moon When Strawberries Are Ripe" and the Omahas call it "Time When Buffalo Bulls Hunt Cows."

JULY

This is "When the Buffalo Bulls Bellow" to the Omahas, "Moon When Geese Shed Their Feathers" to the Dakotas, and "When the Berries Are Ripe" to the Crow.

AUGUST

"When the Elk Bellow" is how the Omahas refer to August, while the Dakotas call it "Harvest Moon." The Pawnees call the time around July and August "Cultivating."

SEPTEMBER

The Dakotas call this "Moon When the Leaves Turn Brown" and the Crows say "When the Leaves Turn Yellow." The Pawnee word for September means "Harvest" and the Omahas say this is "When the Deer Paw the Earth."

OCTOBER

This is "Corn Harvest Moon" to the Dakotas and "When the Leaves Fall" to the Crow. To the Pawnees, October (like September) is "Harvest" and the Omahas say this is "When the Deer Rut."

NOVEMBER

To the Crows November is "When the First Snow Falls"; to the Dakotas, "Winter Moon"; and to the Omaha People, "When the Deer Shed the Antlers." The Pawnee Indians are influenced by the constellations; therefore, one part of November might be called "Big Duck" and the other "Little Duck," depending on the position of the stars in the fall skies.

DECEMBER

The Omaha Indians refer to this month as "When the Little Black Bears Are Born"; the Dakota call it "When the Deer Shed Its Horns." The Pawnees call December Kaata— "Darkness."

Poems of the Plains and Prairie Peoples

A poem speaks of ideas and emotions in a more powerful, more touching way than ordinary speech. Native American poetry is strong, spare, insightful, and filled with appreciation for being alive.

> *At night may I roam*
> *Against the winds may I roam*
> *At night may I roam*
> *When the owl is hooting*
> *May I roam.*
>
> *At dawn may I roam*
> *Against the winds may I roam*
> *At dawn may I roam*
> *When the crow is calling*
> *May I roam.*
>
> —Teton Sioux[2]

> *Because I am poor*
> *I pray for every living creature.*
>
> —Kiowa

Often, heartfelt words were sung rather than spoken. There were songs of mourning, of peace, of thanksgiving, and songs for going into battle; there were planting songs, lullabies, harvest songs, songs to win love, and chants to express hate. Perhaps this rhythmic way of "saying things" influenced American Indian speeches and made them so poetic and powerful.

War Song

> *Here on my breast have I bled!*
> *See-see! there are fighting scars!*
> *Mountains tremble at my yell!*
> *I strike for life!*
>
> —Ojibway[3]

Hunting Song

> *Something I've killed, and I lift up my voice,*
> *Something I've killed, and I lift up my voice,*
> *The mother buffalo I've killed, and I lift up my voice,*
> *Something I've killed, and I lift up my voice.*
>
> —Dakota[4]

I Sing for the Animals

Out of the earth
I sing for them,
A Horse nation
I sing for them.

—Teton Sioux[5]

RIDDLES FROM THE PLAINS AND PRAIRIES

The Plains Indians loved telling jokes[6], many of which were based on puns (plays on words). Their riddles also show them having fun with language.

What sound always makes you feel small?	*Thunder* (Comanche)
What is the strongest animal?	*A skunk* (Comanche)
What is a shining mirror with a house made of pine boughs?	*An eye with its eyelashes* (Plains)
What goes all around your lodge but never comes in?	*A path* (Cherokee)
Who are the ones that always "stand at attention"?	*The lodge cover stakes* (Arapaho)
What never gets tired of motioning for you to come over?	*The top tent flaps* (Arapaho)
What is always running along with no sense?	*A river* (Plains)
Who is the girl that always wears tan paint on her cheeks?	*A raccoon* (Comanche)
What is completely white haired—yet it grows green plumes?	*An onion* (Plains)
What is it that grows fat by sitting down?	*A wood tick* (Plains)
What feels like lightning inside you?	*Meanness* (Comanche)
What is it that for one day always gets its own way?	*A prairie fire* (Comanche)
What two never get tired of moving?	*Your two eyelids* (Plains)
What part of you can travel the fastest?	*Your thoughts* (Arapaho)
What has many little branches—yet it is very light?	*An eagle feather* (Plains)

In addition to spoken languages, early Plains people had other ways of "talking" with one another. These included smoke signals, the way in which a blanket was worn, and, most well known, the use of sign language.

SIGN LANGUAGE

Sign language, created with the hands, probably grew slowly from the concrete (the picture) to the symbolic, which showed the movement, shape or placement of the word within a thought.

Most signs were made at chest level mainly with the right hand. The left hand served to back up or complement the movement of the right.

Among the Shoshoni, elbows bent with hands held up near chest and hands dangling down from the wrists, fingers and thumbs drooping down meant "rainfall"; when this action was done near the eyes, it meant "crying."

Two hands, palms down, extended in front of chest; left hand rubs back and forth across top of right hand at least two times: throughout the Plains this meant an "Indian person."

A right hand doubled into a fist and placed on the forehead meant anger. Both hands clenched and arms crossed at wrists up against the chest meant "love."

To understand sign language required attentiveness as the signs could follow one upon the other very quickly. Warriors used signs during buffalo hunts and when approaching an enemy village. The most expert users were the Teton-Dakota, the Crow, and the Kiowa— who most likely invented it.

The first Europeans to learn sign language were the trappers, the missionaries, and members of the U.S. Army, who used it to communicate with their native scouts.

Some signs are very direct and natural such as the ones that indicate *up, down, you, me, come here,* and *be quiet.*

STORYTELLING

Among the Plains Indians stories became part of the child's psyche through repeated listenings and retellings. Storytelling took place in formalized settings and made use of set rhythmic patterns.[7]

The Plains storyteller began his tale in a specific way, which made clear whether it was set in mythical or historic time and what its importance was. The way he started the story prepared the listener for the kind of tale to come.

Trickster stories that feature Coyote or Saynday teach the listener what skills and powers are necessary for life on earth. There are penalties for disobeying or forgetting the laws of nature, and also for being led into weakness by "trickster" ways. Some of the stories show that, through ceremonies and prayer, people may re-establish their sacred connections.

There are also stories about events said to have taken place "in the living memories of elders of the tribe." These may use references to specific landmarks or dates that appear in the tribe's skin paintings or Winter Counts. They are important because they are the results of generations of retelling of what was once a first-hand account; these stories are a form of Native American oral history.

Eight Tales of the Plains and Prairie Tribes

HOW OLD MAN MADE THE WORLD (CROW)

Long before there was any earth or any people or any animals—except four little ducks—the Creator, who the Crow call Old Man, came up to these four ducks and asked who among them was the bravest.

"Why, I am," replied one of the little ducks.

"Dive down, then, to the bottom of all this water and bring up some mud so that I may see what I can make of it."

The little duck did this and Old Man took the mud in the palm of his hand and let the mud dry there. Then he blew upon the dried mud: he blew the mud to the North and to the South and to the East and to the West, and wherever the mud settled it became hills, valleys, mountains and the prairies of today.

The little duck asked Old Man to make more living things. Old Man took more mud in his hand and when it dried he blew on it—and there stood a living woman and a living man: the first Crow Indians.

Old Man saw that these new creatures would need food and clothes so he had the little duck bring up some more mud and from this he fashioned plants and animals. He killed one of the buffaloes he had made and showed the man and woman how to use it. "Eat the best parts," he said, "to give you strength. The horns can each be a drinking cup; this inner pouch may be used as a bucket; the hide will make a good robe." He showed them how to dress the hide and how to crack the bones to make rich soup.

Then Old Man showed the man and the woman how to make fire, how to make arrowheads and how to make a sweat lodge.

"You will need dreams and visions," he told the man. "Here's how to get them. Go up into the mountains; do not eat anything while you are there. Then cut a piece of flesh off yourself and make an offering of it to me. Soon you will have dreams that will tell you what to do with your life.

"I have given you Crow people the best of the lands I've made. All around you is everything you could need: fresh clear water, plentiful game and plants, and timber for building.

I have not made too many of you because if there were a large number of you, you would be too powerful and you would kill the other people I have made. You Crows are few, but you are brave."

Saynday Tales[8] (Kiowa)

It was him, Saynday, who got it all started; that's what the Kiowas say. He made it all, the good and the not so good. He was a funny looking guy—tall and skinny, with a droopy moustache hanging down over his mouth, and muscles in his arms and legs that looked like little bags of cornmeal. He had this high whiny voice that spoke its own language, but you could tell what he meant 'cause lots of the words were sort of familiar. Saynday lived a long time ago, so all the things I'm tellin' you happened a long time ago too.

The day finally came when Saynday had finished makin' everything in the world, all the good stuff, and the not so good. So, right at sunset, he called together all the animals he'd made. And they all came: Bear and Skunk and Coyote and Deer and Hummingbird and Dragonfly. Why, even Kingsnake and Prairie Dog and Bobcat and Spider Woman were there!

"Well," Saynday said, "I'm done, so I'm goin' to be goin'. I fixed everythin' up the best I could, all except for one thing, and I'm gonna fix that now. See over there in the east, there's one place that don't have no stars." And he stretched his left hand to the east and a bright star appeared at the end of each one of his fingers, and these five stars shot off into the night and filled the empty space in the sky.

"Well, Friends," Saynday said, "it's all finished now, and because I made everything I get to make a few rules and here they are: I want you to tell stories about how I got it all started, but you can only tell these stories during the winter, when the outdoor's work is done. And only tell these stories at night after the day's work is over. Also, always start my stories with the very same words: 'Saynday was comin' along . . . ' If you keep these rules the world will keep on going and if you don't keep these rules, I'll cut off your nose!"

Then Saynday pointed to the place where he had filled the empty space in the sky and said, "Now that's where I'm goin' and I'll always be up there watching to see that you're followin' my rules! All the summer you'll see my five finger stars shinin' in the sky, and when winter comes those stars will disappear, and only *then* can you start to tell my tales. Now I'm goin' away. Good-bye, my friends."

And before a one of them could speak a word, Saynday was gone up into the sky with only his finger stars twinkling to show he was looking down on them.

And that's the way it was then and that's how it is to this very day.

CHILDREN OF THE SUN AND THE MOON (OSAGE)

Time was when some of the Osage lived in the sky. They wanted to know how they got there so they went to the Sun and he said,

"You are my children."

The Osage next went to the Moon and she told them that she was their mother, and that the time had come for them to go live down on earth.

Well, the Osage went on down, but they couldn't live down on the earth because it was covered with water. They felt terrible because now they had no place to call "home." The animals who were with them turned to the noble elk and asked him to help. So the elk lowered himself into the water, but he was so heavy that he began to sink.

"Help me, oh winds of the world! Blow on these waters that I may live!"

And all the winds of the world came and blew upon the waters until they just disappeared into mists.

So the Osage people could walk on the earth at last! At first they saw only rocks and stones covering the land, but after a while soft rich soil came into sight. When the elk saw this fine earth he was filled with joy and he laid down and rolled over and over on the ground to show his happiness. Many of his loose hairs stuck in the earth and each of these grew into a fine plant: corn, squash, beans, potatoes, wild turnips and, finally, all the trees and bushes and grasses that cover our good earth today.

HOW MUSKRAT HELPED (OJIBWAY)

The Ojibways believed that Nanabush was the invisible power who they could meet with in their dreams. Here is one of their stories about Nanabush.

It seems that, after the Great Flood, Muskrat worked hard and helped Nanabush, the Great Spirit, by diving down under the water many times and bringing up loads of mud in his paws. He gave this mud to Nanabush who used it to make the grasslands and channels through which the streams could run their course.

Nanabush wanted to reward Muskrat for his help and so he said to him, "You may choose to live in any place in the world, Muskrat; where do you want to be?"

"I want to live in the deep blue lakes because they are so beautiful," replied Muskrat. But on the very next day he changed his mind and asked to live on the grassy Great Plains. This Nanabush allowed but on the third day, when Muskrat changed his mind again, Nanabush grew annoyed and he said, "You are not happy on water OR on land, so from this day on you will live in the marshes, Muskrat, where it is neither totally wet nor totally dry, and this way you'll never need to change your mind AGAIN!" And so it has been from that day to this!

White Buffalo Woman (Oglala Sioux)

Once two scouts were out looking for buffalo. They came to the top of a hill and looked north. Away off there they saw somebody coming toward them. It was a woman. The one man said, "I'm gonna go and get her!" But the other man said, "I can tell that is a sacred woman. You'd better get rid of all those bad ideas!"

When she came closer they saw how the woman was dressed, in fine white buckskin. Her hair was long and black and silky. She was very beautiful and she could read their minds. In a voice like falling snow she said, "Come to me and do as you will."

The first scout jumped up and ran to the woman. He was going to grab her but when he got near her, all at once, a big white cloud covered them both. After a while the beautiful woman stepped out of the cloud. When the air cleared all that was left of the foolish man was a pile of bleached bones covered with worms!

Then the woman turned to the second man and said, "Go home. Tell your people that I am coming. Put up a big tipi for me in the middle of the Nation."

So the man ran off to tell the people. He was real scared, I can tell you *that*. Quickly the people put up the big tipi and then they waited for the sacred woman.

At last she appeared and came toward them singing these words:

With visible breath I am walking
A voice I am sounding as I walk
In a sacred manner I am walking
With visible tracks I am walking
In a sacred manner I walk.

As she sang a white cloud that smelled like tiny flowers came out of her mouth. She entered the tipi where the Chief of the Sioux awaited her. She handed him a pipe. On it was carved a buffalo that stood for our earth that feeds us. Twelve eagle feathers hung from the stem of the pipe; this stood for the sky and the twelve moons. The feathers were tied to the pipe with a sweet grass that can never break.

"Look," she said, "this will help you grow and be a great nation. Only the hands of those that are good may touch this pipe. Those who are bad will not even be able to see it." Then she sang once again and left the tipi.

The Sioux people watched as she walked off. They saw her become a pure white buffalo that galloped away into the distance.

This they tell and whether it happened so or not I do not know, but if you think about it, you can see that it is true.

How Corn and Buffalo Came to the Cheyenne People

Long, long ago, way back in time, the Cheyenne people were camped around a bubbling spring. They hadn't been able to find any buffalo for meat, but at least that night they had plenty of water to drink.

The following morning there were still no buffalo sighted, and some of the young men began to play the hoop game, a game of skill played with a red and black hoop and four long sticks: two black and two red. The hoop is rolled quickly along the ground and players try to throw their sticks through the moving hoop.

Suddenly two young men appeared from opposite directions, and yet they were dressed exactly alike; their bodies were painted yellow and each wore a yellow breechcloth and a buffalo robe with the hair on the outside, and each had an eagle feather attached to his head.

They came up to one another and the first young man said, "Why are you copying the way I am dressed?"

"I'm not imitating you," said the second young man, *"you* are copying *me!"*

Once they got to talking they learned that they had both gone into the spring and had been told to dress this way. So they determined to enter the spring again, which they did; both disappeared beneath the waters.

They came out on the underside of the spring and went into a cave where an old woman sat next to a fire on which two big clay pots were cooking; one held meat and one held a corn stew.

"Ah, my grandchildren, you've returned," said the old woman. "Good. Come sit by me and eat your fill." Which they did, and though they ate a great deal the two pots were still each full to the brim.

Then the old woman guided their eyes to the south and they saw prairies covered with buffalo. Next they looked to the west and they saw all kinds of animals grazing: deer, elk, antelope, and even horses, which they had never seen before. Then she told them to look north and the two young men saw field after field of tall green corn.

"This will all be yours in the future. I will see to it. Now take these two pots of food to your hungry tribe, and also take this seed corn which you are to plant in the coming spring. Water it well that it may feed your people."

The two young men did as she said, and when they came out of the spring their bodies were painted red and the eagle feathers they wore were bright red also.

All the people ate their fill and only then did the two pots become empty.

That evening the tribe watched in astonishment as, from the spring, one after another, there emerged an enormous herd of buffalo! They continued coming out of the spring all that night and in the morning the people found the land filled with the huge brown beasts.

Now there was plenty of meat for the people. In the spring of the year they moved their camp to a valley and planted the seeds the old woman had sent them. Lovely tall corn stalks grew and each stalk held two to four ears of corn. After that the Cheyennes planted corn every year.

One year they returned from a hunt to find that someone had stolen every ear of corn from their fields, and though they searched everywhere they never found the thieves. After that it was many years before the Cheyenne farmed again.

Coyote and the Rock (White River Sioux)

"Mitakuye-Oyassin!⁹ All my relations!"

Coyote was walking along with Iktome, the Sioux Spider Man. All of a sudden they saw this fine big rock with lines of moss all over it—the kind that tells a story! This rock was Iya, and Iya has power!

"Say, that is one fine rock!" said Coyote. "I'm going to give it my thick new blanket," and he laid the blanket over the stone. "Now you won't be cold anymore."

"Wow, Coyote! I didn't know you were so generous!" said Iktome.

"Ah, sure," replied Coyote. "I'm always giving away my stuff."

So Coyote and Iktome walked on a way. Now the sun went down and Coyote began to shiver.

"Hey, I'm gettin' cold," complained Coyote. "I'm goin' back and get my blanket."

"Wait a minute," said Iktome, "you can't do that 'cause that's not *your* blanket anymore. You gave it to the rock, remember? And *that* rock's got strong medicine—you'd better not fool with it."

"Well, rocks don't need blankets after dark and I do, so I'm goin' and gettin' mine back." And Coyote trotted back to Iya.

"I'm takin' back my blanket now 'cause I'm freezin' to death," he told the stone.

"You can't do that—what's given is given!" responded Iya.

At this, Coyote ripped the blanket off the stone, wrapped it around himself and trotted back to the cave where Iktome was waiting for him. When he got inside the cave, Coyote heard something.

"What's that noise, Iktome?" Coyote asked, and sure enough they could hear a roar and it was getting louder and louder. They both looked outside and even in the dark they could see that it was Iya, roaring down the hill right toward them!

"Let's get outta here!" screamed Coyote, and the two friends tore off! Through the night, across the river, into the woods, out onto the plains—and all that time that big old rock was right on their heels!!

Then Iktome stopped short and said, "This isn't *my* fight, Bro. I'm outta here!" and with that Iktome curled up into a ball and turned back into a spider and ran down a little mouse hole.

On and on Coyote raced until at last Iya, with a thrust of speed, caught up with the Trickster and rolled right over him. Then the rock ripped the blanket away from Coyote and left him laying there, smashed flat.

"Like I said, Coyote, what's given is GIVEN!" and Iya rolled on back to his home.

Just then a white rancher rode up and took the flattened Coyote home for a rug. Now, Coyote has the gift to bring himself back to life when he is killed, but *this* time it wasn't that easy and it was almost noon when the rancher's wife yelled out to her husband, "Honey, there goes your new rug hightailin' it off to the woods!"

So it is, Friends: a gift must come from the heart, and once given it remains so—forever!

STOLEN GIRL (CHEYENNE)

Once there was a young girl whose father was a chief. She had many, many admirers, and more than one young man had asked her to marry him. But she would not have any of them. She was waiting to marry someone she loved.

Then one night, while lying on her buffalo robe, the girl smelled a delightful scent. With an awl she poked a hole in the lodge skins and looked through it; outside she could make out the figure of a young man. She liked his looks and she was curious, as he was clearly a stranger, so she got up and slipped outside to speak with him.

They talked together for a long while, during which the girl asked his name.

"Red Eye is my name," he said. "My home is far to the East from here. Come with me and we shall go to the lodge of my father!"

The girl loved the way he spoke to her and, so, she went back into her lodge to get a few things to take with her to her new life; she gathered up her awl, some sinews and her quills and put them all in a leather pouch.

"I live away to the East. Come. By nightfall we shall be in our new home," Red Eye told her.

Finally they arrived at a wooded place where his camp was pitched. They went up to the big lodge standing in the middle. Through the skins they could see the outlines of many men sitting around a fire.

The two young people entered and when the chief, Red Eye's father, saw them he said, "Oh, my son, you have returned with your bride. How happy we are to see you here together."

The young girl went over and sat on the women's side. She felt relieved to be at her destination at last. As she sat there she noticed, in the flickering light, the beautiful paintings on the tent linings; she saw that the lodge was richly furnished—and she also noted to herself that all of the men of this tribe had quite long pointed noses.

Back at the camp, where this girl's parents were, there was great excitement and sadness. Her father was so upset at the loss of his daughter that he promised that she would marry whoever could find her. All the young men began to search wildly for her.

Now, when the young girl awakened in the morning, she realized that she was not lying on a fine buffalo robe. Instead, she found herself sitting on a pile of dried grass in a hollow tree and all around her scampered mountain rats. That's how one of the young men out looking for her saw her, crawling out of that hollow tree trunk.

"We have been so worried, young woman. People back home are crying ever since you left."

"Friend," she replied, "I was stolen by rats and brought to this tree."

(This, they say, shows how mountain pack rats first began taking things from people, long ago.)

Then the young man who found her took the girl back to her father's lodge and quite soon after this they were married.

How the World Ends (White River Sioux)

Somewhere hidden away at that place where the prairie and Maka Sicha—the Badlands—meet, there is a cave. *Nobody* who is alive today knows where this cave is.

In the cave lives a withered old woman. She wears a buckskin dress like we used to wear before the white men came. She sits in that cave weaving a blanket strip of colored porcupine quills for her buffalo robe. Every quill she uses is flattened by chewing it, and that is why this ancient woman's teeth are worn down to little stumps; she has been working on this strip for over a thousand years.

A huge black dog, his name is Shunka Sape, lies at her feet. A crackling fire is blazing at the back of the cave. The old woman built the fire ten centuries ago and she's never let it go out. Over the fire hangs a clay pot, the kind we used before white traders brought iron kettles to our land, and in this pot bubbles "wojapi," a rich sweet berry soup. This soup has been boiling in that pot for as long as the fire has been burning.

Whenever the old lady gets up to stir the soup, the big black dog immediately begins pulling out the porcupine quills from her blanket strip. He rapidly undoes the weaving until the moment when the ancient one turns to come back to her work. Then he lies down again. This happens over and over, hour by hour, day after week after year. So it is that the old woman never ever quite finishes her weaving. The Sioux people believe that if the old woman *ever* finishes her blanket strip—at that last second when she weaves the last porcupine quill into place and completes the design—our world will come to an end!

Notes for "Language"

1. The "moons" and other time periods mentioned in this section are not identical with the months in our modern calendar; the match-ups in the list are rough approximations. We have a similar situation in our own calendar: Easter falls in March in some years and in April in others.

2. Appeared in *Teton Sioux Music* by Frances Densmore. From Bureau of American Ethnology Bulletin No. 61. Reprinted by permission of the Smithsonian Institution.

3. From *Ojibwa Songs*, by H.H. Schoolcraft.

4. Translated by Stephen Riggs. Reprinted by permission of the Smithsonian Institution.

5. Appeared in *Teton Sioux Music* by Frances Densmore. From Bureau of American Ethnology Bulletin No. 61. Reprinted by permission of the Smithsonian Institution.

6. The Plains people also loved to tell little stories similar to "tall tales," which were funny because of extreme exaggerations, unexpected comparisons, and silly situations. Often they told these stories with completely straight faces—as this only added to the humor of the tales!

7. The Kiowas had a set of stories just for summer that would be told during their Sun Dance. These were sacred tales and could only be told by certain special storytellers, and in *exactly* the same way each time.

8. Sayday stories are still told to Kiowa children in Oklahoma. In fact, each year new Sayday tales appear featuring contemporary objects and events. It goes to show that, after all these many years, Sayday is *still* "comin' along"!

9. The Siouan phrase "Mitakuye-Oyassin" means "all my relations" and is spoken to remind the listener that all things on Earth are of one family, related to everything in the natural world. It is used to signal that something very serious, important, or sacred is about to be shared with the listeners.

   When a Lakota storyteller begins with "Ehanni" and really draws it out (Eha-a-a-a-a-a-a-a-a-a-a-a-nni), it is the same as saying "a long, long, long, long time ago" or "In the beginning . . ." This means you are about to hear a tale about things that took place before the world was even created. If the storyteller begins with a somewhat shortened "Eha-a-a-nni," it means that these events took place long ago, but not that long ago, and the tale is not as sacred nor as serious. In these "more recent" stories the gods are retreating and people begin to appear on Earth; in these stories people often are learning how to deal with their new existence.

ARTS AND CRAFTS

MUSIC

Music was a part of the daily life of the Plains Indian. Their music was not written down. Each song was memorized individually. There were songs for every part of life: work, play, falling asleep, being in love; songs of competition, hunting, war and death; as well as songs to celebrate being alive on this very beautiful day.[1]

Native American music has rhythm, melody, and harmony. *Rhythm* is felt in our breathing, in the dripping of water, in our very pulses. Life is rhythmic. *Melody* is a series of sounds of different pitch: bird songs, the howl of a coyote, the laughter of a young woman. *Harmony* is the blending together of several sounds; in nature we hear combined sounds when the wind blows through the boughs and leaves of the trees, and when rain falls on the tipi cover as we warm ourselves by the crackling fire within.

Singing was believed to have the power to put a person in perfect balance with all of nature.

Their music was extremely personal and was made as prayers for ancestors, for good hunting, safety, rain, and to note the changing seasons.

Plains songs were sung loudly, with gusto, strong rhythms, and long-held tones. Often music was connected with warfare, religious and military ceremonies. Songs brought power and every medicine man had his own songs. Many times songs were received in visions and they could be sold or given away, but no one could simply take such a song.

Each warrior composed his own death song so that, in the event that he was captured, he might die while singing this unique song.

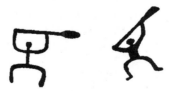

THE VISUAL ARTS

The early Plains and Prairie peoples showed their artistry in the designs on their tent covers and linings, their clothing, and their tools. They excelled in quillwork, the carving of stone pipes, and in painted decorations.

65

Quillwork

In North America this craft was practiced primarily by Sioux, Mandan, Hidatsa, Kiowa, Cheyenne, and Arapaho women. The men were responsible for hunting the porcupines and birds[2] from which the quills were gotten. In some tribes the men prepared the dyes from roots, bark, buds and plants, while the women sorted, flattened and applied the colorful quills to the deerskin or hide.

The largest porcupine quills came from the tail of the animal; somewhat smaller, though still big, were the ones that came from the back. Small quills came from the neck and the finest were found on the rest of the animal's body.

First, the quills were soaked and softened in water and then they were dyed. Red, yellow, green, blue, and black were the usual colors. Feather quills were split up to the tip with an awl. Then the quills were all sorted by size.

In the next step, a woman would hold several quills in her mouth to again soften them. She would draw each one between her teeth to flatten it. The flattened quills were sewn or woven into clothing, including belts, garters, leggings, wristguards, shirts, moccasins, and dresses. They were also applied as decoration on bags, boxes, toys, balls, and weapons.

In one method the quill designs were held in place with sinew threads and one to three stitches.

Another method was to apply the decorations to clothing, pipe stems and feather shafts, using the wrapping technique.

Wrapped

Sometimes strips of rawhide were quilled and used as bands within a design; this gave a firmer finished object and was practical for use on breastplates, wristguards, and knee and arm bands.

Rosettes often were used as quilled decorations on dresses and robes.

Rosette

Quill plaiting was a common technique practiced by the Mandans, Sioux, Poncas, Hidatsas, and Cheyennes.

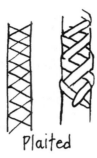

Plaited

A quill presser made of bone or horn was used to give a final flattening to the quills once they were sewn or woven in place.

Quillwork is an art invented by Native Americans and is produced nowhere else in the world!

Photo 13. Petalasharo, Chief of the Pawnee; circa 1871. *Photo by William H. Jackson. Courtesy Museum of New Mexico (neg. no. 58635).*

<u>HOW DOUBLE WOMAN BROUGHT QUILLING TO THE LAKOTA SIOUX</u>

Once a young Lakota girl had a dream. In the dream a woman—who was really twins—came to her. This was Double Woman and she showed the girl how to get quills from a porcupine, how to sort them by length, and how to dye them. Next, Double Woman showed her the sacred designs and how to flatten each quill and weave it into these designs.

All this time the young woman stayed in her tipi while learning this new art of quilling. When at last she came out of her lodge, she went and showed her best friend how to quill. Then she taught the women of the dream societies this new art. From then on only women who had had the honor of being visited by Double Woman in their dreams would be allowed to quill. This work has always been considered more than just a craft; it is thought of as a sacred task.

Bone Work

<u>THE HAIRPIPE BREASTPLATE NECKLACE</u>

Hairpipes (long thin beads made from animal bone) were originally worn by threading one's hair through them; that is how they got their name.

To make a hairpipe necklace, two rows of forty or more bones were strung horizontally between vertical strips of leather; round beads were often strung on these leather thongs. (See Photo 14.)

As it was quite difficult in early times to accumulate the eighty or more thin bones, these necklaces or breastplates were, at first, very costly. Both men and women wore them; a man's reached from neck to waist and a woman's reached below her waist—sometimes down to her ankles!

Photo 14. Apiatou, Kiowa. *Courtesy Museum of New Mexico (neg. no. 86986).*

Painted and Carved Decorations

The Plains and Prairie tribes painted on leather shelters, clothing, weapons, as well as on their own faces and bodies! They painted designs, historical records, and announcements.

BUFFALO HIDE CLOAKS

Many of the Plains Indians wore buffalo hide cloaks that were decorated with elaborate paintings.

To begin making such a cloak, the craftsman first treated the dressed skin with a clear sizing of a glue-like liquid. This would preserve the original color of the hide itself and would hold the color of the painted decorations even after the leather became dirty with use.

After applying the sizing, the craftsman scratched an outline of the proposed design onto the hide and then, using a bone or wood tool, he applied the paint.

Both women and men worked on decorating these cloaks. Among the designs painted mainly by men were those that are called "pictographs": pictures recording events, such as important battles.

The men also did another kind of painting; it derived from the dream world and was believed to have supernatural powers. This type of design was used on war shields.

Women, on the other hand, usually painted highly stylized abstract designs, or completely decorative patterns. An example of this was the feathered circle, which was painted by women on warriors' cloaks to symbolize their war honors; such a cloak would be worn much as combat ribbons are worn today.

Women also painted their abstract designs on parfleches and other personal possessions. (See "Parfleche" in Tools.)

MEDICINE SHIELDS

These shields were circular, about two feet in diameter, and made from the breast or underneck of the bull buffalo. The skin was smoked, allowed to contract to the desired thickness, and then shaped by staking the wet hide over a mound of earth.[3]

The design on the outside cover(s) was (were) different from that on the shield. The design on the shield was often given to an old warrior in a medicine dream. The shield had to be made exactly as shown in the dream in keeping with the wishes of the Shield Spirit, which might be an animal, bird or a deity of the tribe. The shield was seldom made by its owner; it was the dreamer who made it, in secret, and then traded it for blankets and other objects.

Each shield had one or two coverings of soft-dressed buffalo, deer or elk skin that covered the main design until it was ready to be revealed in battle. The medicine shield was a brave's most prized possession. Sometimes a family shield was handed down from father to son and, because it had built up great medicine over the years (by protecting several members of a family), it was especially valued.

TIPI COVERS

Plains tipis were sometimes painted with sacred symbols or scenes of warfare.

Photo 15. A Piegan play tipi; 1926. *Photo by Edward S. Curtis. Courtesy Museum of New Mexico (neg. no. 143852).*

A hired designer would sketch in the symbols on the tipi cover while the owner, using a buffalo bone brush, would often paint in the appropriate colors. The Kiowa of the southern Plains and the Blackfeet of the northern Plains were famous for their tipi cover paintings.

Here is an explanation of Blackfeet symbols as shown on their tipi covers:

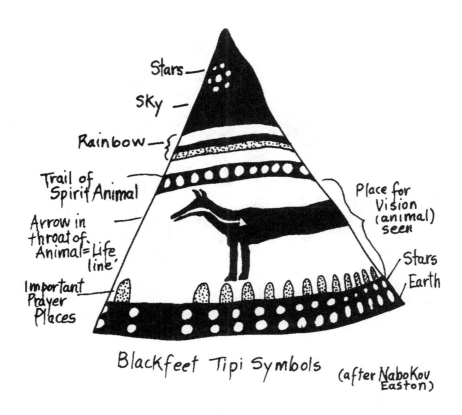

Blackfeet Tipi Symbols (after Nabokov Easton)

TIPI LININGS

Such linings were usually painted in brilliant colors with designs that noted past events in the lives of those who lived in the tipi.

WINTER COUNTS

The Winter Count was a calendar-like device used by the the Kiowa and Sioux. It measured time by winters rather than by European years and is the most extensive North American historical record known. Each year was represented by one pictograph or glyph painted on the tanned side of a buffalo hide. Each glyph was a simple representation of a person, place, or event of that year.

A Winter Count could also be used to record the outstanding events of a family or of a man's life. The old method of painting started with the first symbol (e.g., the birth of the man himself) at the center of the hide. The next picture to be considered was to the left, and one continued "reading" the record in a circling spiral in that direction. The later method of painting these records was linear: reading from left to right and from top to bottom.

LODGE MURALS

Often described as the most spectacular of all Plains painting, these designs decorated the walls of lodges of tribal chiefs and war leaders. Such designs came directly from visions and were believed to be supernaturally powerful. Although an artist would paint these designs, he would be extremely careful to follow the exact directions given to the dreamer to insure that the inherent magic would indeed work.

CARVED STONE PIPES

The Plains tribes went to a sacred stone quarry in present-day Minnesota to collect the blood red, pale pink, or reddish brown stones called "catlinite." This quarry was neutral ground where no fighting was allowed while the men were collecting the stones for pipe-making. Catlinite, or pipestone, is soft enough to be carved and drilled easily.

Pipe bowls were also carved from green serpentine, red argillite, steatite, shale, and limestone. The stems for these pipes were often made from sumac or ash, woods that are easy to hollow out and carve.

Nearly every Plains man owned his own pipe, which he used on religious as well as daily occasions. But the most prized and protected of pipes were the most elaborately decorated and delicately carved. These were believed to be the most powerful pipes and were honored by their owners and stored in beautifully quilled bags. (See "Crafts—Pipestone Pipes" in Activities.)

Notes for "Arts and Crafts"

1. A good way for students to become familiar with Plains music is by listening to tapes while doing puzzles, painting, coloring, or playing quiet indoor games. (See the **Teacher's Resource Guide** for specific sources of Plains Indian tapes.)

2. When speaking of quillwork we usually think of porcupine quills, but the quills of bird feathers were also used—especially to cover large surfaces. The pithy center of feather quills took native dyes better than porcupine quills. In some early brown quillwork, even the stems of maidenhair ferns were used.

3. Lighter weight shields were also made for use in religious ceremonies.

CHILDREN AND PLAY

CHILDREN

A newborn child[1] was immediately bathed, whether it was winter or summer; its navel was lightly coated with puff ball powder to facilitate healing, and the baby was given over to a wet nurse until the mother's strength returned. The baby's umbilical cord was kept in a little quilled bag shaped like a turtle to symbolize long life. Herbs were also put in the bag, which was kept as a life-long sacred charm.

Because a crying baby could frighten away game or alert an enemy, Plains babies were taught from birth not to make loud noises. As soon as a baby cried, an adult would gently hold the child's nose and, because an unweaned baby breathes only through his nose, he would quickly learn to be quiet.

A baby rode in a beautiful warm secure cradleboard on its mother's back. When necessary, the cradleboard could be hung from a branch or set in a safe place while the mother weeded the garden or prepared a buffalo hide.

Young children wore little or no clothing until they were three or four years old. Then a girl might be given a dress very much, in style, like those worn by her mother. A boy began wearing a loin cloth at about eight or nine years of age, and this occasion was greeted with much rejoicing.

Adults treated children with respect, never ridiculing them or taunting them. Corrections were made with great patience, over and over again. Physical discipline was very seldom used. Instead, parents listened to their children, reasoned with them, and finally allowed experience to be the child's teacher.

Children were shown how to eat properly and were encouraged to be serious, honest, modest, and polite. The elders told them that they must live correctly if they wanted to have a life of good fortune. When one of them misbehaved, the other children shunned and admonished him, as they had been taught to do.

Plains children were also made to understand that there were certain things that must not be asked for (and that could not, in turn, be given) because they were forbidden by religious law; such requests risked offending the spirits.

Each child had a special place to put her or his toys. If a child was untidy and left toys strewn around, these would be swept into the garbage pit and the playthings would not be replaced for a long while. Because almost everything was shared within a camp, children seldom quarreled about personal possessions.

At about the age of four the girls began to help their mothers with such household chores as fetching water (three times a day), sweeping, hoeing, cooking, and sewing. They were given play dishes, bits of hide to tan, dolls, quillwork to use on the doll's clothes, tiny cradleboards, and little tipis in which to play.

Photo 16. Nez Perce children at a play tipi; 1899. *Photo by Harry J. Allyn. Courtesy Museum of New Mexico (neg. no. 147445).*

Boys listened to hunting tales and practiced their marksmanship with small bows and blunt arrows that they started using when they were about four years old. No boy was allowed to aim at another child or at an adult. If he did, his toys were taken away from him until he was capable of more appropriate behavior. Every boy anxiously awaited the day of his first real hunt and understood that this day would not come until he could prove he was able to shoot well and handle his weapon in a responsible way.

Young males learned the art of public speaking by attending council meetings with their fathers and uncles. Later, the boys would imitate different speeches they had heard at the meetings.

Each group of Plains people had specific ways of marking a child's life as he or she passed from youth to adulthood. (See the notes for **The Buffalo** section for a description of a Teton Sioux coming-of-age ceremony.)

PLAY

Throughout the year boys and girls usually played separately, understanding early that their roles in life were different. Both boys and girls played competitive sports: racing, jumping, swimming, and climbing.

Photo 17. Hoop dancers Bobby Lujan, Albert Lujan, and Juanita Lujan; 1925. *Courtesy Museum of New Mexico (neg. no. 90741).*

The boys played at tracking and fighting wars, and the outstanding "warrior" soon became the leader of any group. The girls played shinny, homemaker, or went berry picking and so learned to identify many plants.

Photo 18. Sioux boys' first foot race, Standing Rock Agency, North Dakota; circa 1900. *Photo by Keystone View Co. Courtesy Museum of New Mexico (neg. no. 90542).*

Hoop and Stick Game

In early spring the boys played this game—but only for a few weeks. One team threw sinew-laced hoops into the air while the other team tried to catch these hoops on their sticks.

"The rule was," explained Goodbird, son of Buffalo Bird Woman, "that when the ice broke on the Missouri River, we should all go to the high bank over the river and hurl our hoops into the current. We boys were taught, and we really believed it, that these hoops became dead buffaloes after they had passed out of sight around the next point of land . . . . Many dead buffaloes came floating down the Missouri in the springtime and their flesh was much valued."

Ball

Using a ball made of tanned hide stuffed with grass, sewn with sinew and decorated with quillwork, a young Cheyenne girl would compete to see how many times she could bounce the ball on her toe without its touching the ground.

A group of girls might use a larger ball, throwing it up in the air and then catching it alternately on their knees and feet, keeping it moving, again, without letting it touch the earth.

Ball and Stick Game (Shinny)

Played by two teams of young girls, the object of this game was to get the ball past each other's goal. The teams used a shinny stick and a hair-filled leather ball; the use of hands was not allowed. Children learned to play this "hockey" game at about seven or eight years of age.

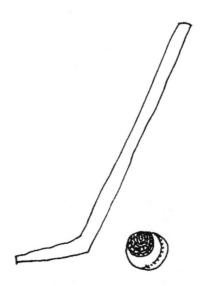

Tops and Whips

Boys would clean off a circular spot on the ground and play with tops made of buffalo horn. They would keep their tops spinning by lashing them with their buckskin whips. The tops were often filled with tallow to give them balance and weight.

Sticks Game (í'-a-ki-hee-kee)

When the boys heard the first thunder of spring they knew it was time for the Sticks Game (í-a-ki-hee-kee)! Long sticks were thrown against the ground to see whose would bounce the furthest. The winner in each round would take the losers' sticks. Each boy made his own playing sticks by peeling the bark off branches and then decorating them as he liked.

SEASONAL PLAY

As we have seen the boys played the Hoop and Stick Game in spring. During the summer they played war against one another, trying to outmaneuver the other team and take its position. Mud balls, which were used for ammunition, were propelled through the air with five- or six-foot willow wands. A mud ball could fly as far as a hundred yards (the length of a modern football field) and, as described by Goodbird, " . . . would hit the boy on the face or body, impacting with a 'splat' and very often making the boy cry."

The girls did not play war games in the summer, but rather spent time making objects and figures out of soft mud, or playing "Follow the Leader," winding their line in and out among the lodges.

As the weather changed, girls would sit inside playing in the yellow sunspot that came down on the floor through the smoke hole. They put away their mud and rush dolls and began to play with beautiful deerskin dolls artfully made for them by affectionate relatives.

After the harvest, boys might go to the river and build a bonfire of corncobs. Then they would press embers into mud balls and hurl these over the water. As the balls fell, they must have looked like showers of falling stars in the darkness of an evening.

In winter the children went sledding, at first using a hide on which to coast downhill. But hides could not build up as much speed as a sled made of buffalo ribs. Five ribs would be connected at one end with wooden slats and at the other with a leather thong threaded through holes bored in the bones; a hide strap was attached to the front to be used in pulling the sled back up the hill.

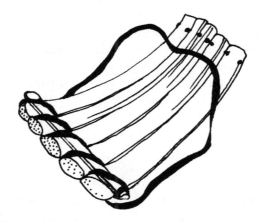

"I look back upon my childhood as the happiest time of my life."
—BUFFALO BIRD WOMAN

Note for "Children and Play"

1. If, at birth, a child was imperfectly formed, it was immediately put to death. This was not thought cruel, as in tribal life each person had to be able to work and give help and food to the others in the group.

   If a child was maimed later in life, he or she was given tender care by everyone in the tribe.

RELIGION

To the Plains Indians religion was not a separate part of their lives; it was present at all times in all things. The Sioux chief Standing Bear said in 1933, "We were surrounded with the blessings of the Great Mystery." This unseen force was stronger than humans and could change their lives. People needed this power in order to find food and win battles. The Sioux called this force Wakonda, Great Mystery, or Great Powers.

In addition to the Great Spirit, some tribes believed that there were living spirits in all natural things as well. One way to be in touch with this powerful unseen world was through the help of a guardian animal, or a guardian spirit.

THE VISION QUEST

When boys—and in some tribes, girls—came of age, at about twelve or thirteen, they went through an initiation ceremony to help them find their own guardian spirit. The young person walked off to a remote place and stayed without food, water, or sleep for four days until, with luck, a personal helper came in a dream or vision. This spirit would protect the boy or girl later in life, whenever there was any serious danger. From a vision a young man might also learn songs, dances, chants or designs that were his personal medicine.

MEDICINE MEN

A strong vision could lead someone to become a medicine man, a person with special gifts for telling the future, giving news from far away, and diagnosing illness. He would be trained in the use of healing plants, and learn how to set bones, stop a hemorrhage, and remove arrows.

Medicine men were counted on to help prevent illness and disaster and to bring victory in battle. Because of their visions, their gifts and their knowledge of songs and prayers, they were thought of as bridges between this world and the spirit world. Other names used for such healers were Mystery Man and The Wonderful.

MEDICINE BUNDLES

A Plains Indian person might make several vision quests during a lifetime. After a vision, objects from it would be put together in a bundle that was expected to protect its owner for life.

Tribes also had such medicine bundles, containing a collection of objects believed to have special powers for the whole community. In one of these bundles you might find a wooden bowl, animal or bird skins, skulls, claws, tobacco, herbs or roots, dried crickets or lizards, oddly shaped stones, a pipe. Such a medicine bundle was opened and used only on ceremonial occasions.

The power of a bundle was meant to be tested—in war, hunting, healing, in love, or in making contact with the spirits. Testing a bundle only made it more powerful!

THE SACRED PIPE AND TOBACCO

The pipe and the tobacco for it had a very important place in Plains Indian ceremonies. There were strict rules as to who could light the pipe and how it was done. There was a certain way to hold it and to pass it around and to keep it when it wasn't being used.

> "Animal Person said [in my vision] I must always lay my pipe on a buffalo chip, for the buffalo was a sacred animal, and that when I prayed, blowing smoke to the four directions of the world, to those above, and to our mother (earth), my prayers would have more power."

—J. W. SCHULTZ[1]

It was a great honor to have a ceremonial pipe bundle; it could also be expensive, as the one who held the bundle had to provide a feast for everyone whenever the pipe was used in a ceremony.

Many of the ancient Plains pipes that have been found are decorated with carvings of animals or fish.

SWEAT BATHS

Most Native American tribes used sweat baths for religious reasons (see **Shelters**). They helped people be more healthy, both in body and mind.

SACRED CEREMONIES

In their ceremonies the Plains Indians honored the Great Spirit and the spirits of the natural world, in the hope that these powers would continue to provide them with rain, food, safety, and success. By their participation, the people reinforced the values and religious beliefs of the tribe.

Not all ceremonies included the whole tribe; some were just for women, or just for men, or just for one honored person. There were secret ceremonies in which only the dancers and a medicine man participated. Some ceremonies were performed yearly, always on the same day.[2]

Buffalo Dance

Each summer the roaming Plains bands that made up a tribe would come together and place their tipis in a circle. This marked the beginning of the buffalo hunt. Sacred dances were performed before the hunt, as the Plains people believed that this ceremony would bring the bison herds to them. These dances lasted until the buffalo were sighted, which could be three days or three weeks. When one of the dancers grew too tired to continue, the others would pretend to kill him and cut up his "carcass" as if he were a bison himself.

The buffalo was so much a part of the circle of life for the Sioux that they believed that when the buffalo was gone, the Indians, themselves, would disappear.

The Medicine Feast

After the hunt the very best of the game was cooked and offered to the Great Mystery; this was called The Medicine Feast.

"As a woman lowered the boiling pot or the fragrant roast of venison ready to serve, she would first whisper, 'Great Mystery, do thou partake of this venison, and still be gracious!' This was the commonly said grace."

—CHIYESA, AN 18TH-CENTURY SANTEE SIOUX

Hako Ceremony

The Pawnee Hako ceremony was five days long and was held in order to place the children under the protection of the corn and the eagle. During this ritual, the people prayed for peace among the tribes. This ceremony involved a parade across the lands between the various camps.

The Sun Dance Ceremony

The Sun (Gaze) Dance was the main ceremony of the Plains Indians, meant to renew the earth and to celebrate life. It was performed so that a participant might have a vision or fulfill a promise made to a spirit during a time of great danger. One of the most common prayers said during the ceremony was the plea to keep lightning—which was so dangerous on the prairies—from striking the Plains Indian camps and people.

The tribe gathered together in mid-summer.[3] They put up a Sun Pole, Sun Lodge, and made the Sun Trail that led to it. It took four days to build the lodge (see **Shelters**); the second four days, the ceremony itself took place.

Photo 19. Cheyenne Sun Dance pledgers; 1911. *Photo by Edward S. Curtis. Courtesy Museum of New Mexico (neg. no. 65118).*

Then came for the Mandan, the Okipa, the ceremony that stood for a man's struggles to overcome pain and to keep his mind on thoughts of the spirit. The men who had agreed to take part were "captured" by members of the Buffalo Society (see **Social Order and Government**). They were tied up and tormented by other tribal members; this included being tortured by having pointed sticks roughly stuck through the muscles of their backs, chests, or shoulder blades. All this time they could not show any signs of pain and were encouraged to laugh at their torturers.

Two wooden skewers were pushed through the chest muscles of each man and leather thongs were tied to the skewers. The thongs were then pulled and jerked, either by the man himself or by others. The free end of each thong was tied to a stick that was then thrown over the crossbars of the Sun Pole; members of the group sometimes pulled down on these handles until the stretched thongs lifted the brave off his feet and he was left dangling overhead, held up by the two skewers in his chest. While hanging like this, the man blew through an eagle-bone whistle and stared continually at the sun. From time to time he would be lowered to the ground so that he might rest a bit. If a man were to give up and quit in the middle of the Sun Dance ceremony, he would be totally disgraced in the eyes of his people.

During all these trials the other tribe members sang ceremonial songs. From time to time they would pull on the thongs in an effort to help the suspended man tear free from the skewers, for *that* was the high point of the Sun Dance—the moment when a man fell back to earth and, hopefully, received his vision!

Once the ceremony was over the Sun Lodge was taken down, leaving only the undecorated Sun Pole standing alone out in the plains.

To us today, the Sun Gaze Dance may sound very harsh, but we need to remember that the Plains people led very hard lives and they had to be strong and brave in order to survive. The men needed to be able to overcome bodily pain and to prove their courage and strength: these were important reasons for them to have taken part in this Sun Dance ceremony.

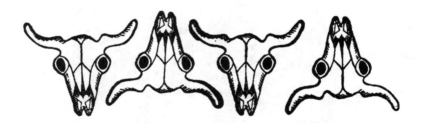

DEATH AND THE AFTERLIFE

On the whole, early Plains people saw death as part of the natural cycle. They mourned the death of close ones and respectfully prepared their bodies so the spirits of the dead could make the journey to the afterlife in the Spirit World.

The Cheyennes, for example, believed that the dead walked the Milky Way to where the Chief—the Creator, the Wise One Above—awaited. Everyone, good and bad alike, went there; everyone, the Cheyenne said, was equal after death. There was no reward there for having led a good life and no punishment for those who had fallen short. In the afterlife you hunted, ate, slept, and warred just as you did on earth.

Among the Wichita Indians, when a man died, his body was dressed well and painted and kept at home until a grave had been dug on some nearby hill. The digging of the grave was done by a person chosen to carry out the burial; later, this person was adopted into the family of the deceased. The body was laid out full length and the man's warring tools, except for his shield, were put in the grave. The entire village mourned for four days, followed by a ceremony in the mourning lodge.

The Wichita believed that the soul went to Spirit-land, where the old life was relived in complete happiness.

When an Assiniboin or Hidatsa man died, his body was dressed well, wrapped in robes along with his special tools or weapons—which might be needed in the next world—and then put on a high wooden table, or scaffold, out on the plains. (Some tribes placed the wrapped corpse high in a tree.) The person's head was always laid to the east. Afterwards the Hidatsa clan fathers and aunts would stop by beneath the platform and say a few words to the body.

"My son," they would say, "I wish you to go to the Ghost Land right away. Do not remain here, or try to harm anyone in the village, but go at once to the Ghost Land . . . ."

When, after many months, the wooden platform weakened and collapsed, the Assiniboin people collected the bones of the different bodies—all except for the skulls, which they arranged in a circle around a medicine pole on the empty land. This circle was called "the village of the dead." It was visited by the tribes-people so they might talk with the dead and leave them small gifts.

It was the rule among the Sioux and many other Plains tribes that, once the wrapped body was placed above the ground , the nearest relatives stood guard beside the platform for two days and a night. The closest woman relative kept up a wailing cry for this entire time. Food and gifts were left nearby so that the spirit could use them on its way to the next world. Once this period of mourning was over, the people went away and never came back to that place again.

What is life? It is a flash of a firefly at night. It is the breath of a buffalo in the winter time. It is the little shadow which runs across the grass and loses itself in the sunset.

—A 19TH-CENTURY CROWFOOT[4]

So it was that the Plains Indians observed the natural world closely. They tried to understand its cycles and its power. They prayed to the spirits of this natural world and accepted from them whatever they might be offered.

Notes for "Religion"

1. *My Life as an Indian*, page 151.

2. A large wheel-shaped structure, eighty feet across, is found near the top of Big Horn mountain in Wyoming. It is called the Medicine Wheel and has twenty-eight spokes. Astronomers suggest that this was a basic observatory with which the Plains Indians could identify the exact time of the summer solstice and the correct times of their yearly ceremonies.

3. The Sun Dance was occasionally held in the fall.

4. As quoted on page 274 of *The Way to Independence* by Carolyn Gilman and Mary Jane Schneider, published by Minnesota Historical Society, 1986.

TRADE

There was a rich pattern of inter-tribal trading among the Plains peoples. Most of it took place between the farmers and the hunting people, which was good for both groups. (There wasn't as much reason for farming people to trade with other crop-growers.)

The nomadic tribes offered dried meats, dressed hides, buffalo robes, deerskin clothing decorated with feathers, quillwork, and painted objects. In exchange they received pemmican, beans, nuts, corn, pumpkins, squash, or wild plants; depending on the season, these were offered fresh or dried.

Because the tribes along the Missouri River, such as the Mandan, lived in permanent lodges, their villages became busy trade centers.

The Plains Apaches took deerskin and hides for shoes as far away as New Mexico, where they traded them to the Rio Grande Pueblo peoples in return for corn, cotton, and hair blankets.

Tribes that were distant from one another and had different languages were able to trade by using go-betweens. The Crow, for example, helped goods flow between the Hidatsa and the Nez Perce.

The Nez Perce corn husk bags were traded for dried vegetables—and, in some cases, might be exchanged for instruction in a ceremonial ritual or dance!

SOCIAL ORDER AND GOVERNMENT

GOVERNMENT

The Plains Indians were divided into tribes,[1] and these were made up of clans[2] or bands,[3] each with a chief and his followers.[4] Within a tribe no clan had more power than any other. The Cheyenne tribe, for example, was divided into ten main bands. Four chiefs from each band and four central chiefs made up the governing body of the Cheyenne—The Council of 44. This was an elected group and was represented by a special symbol—a set of four sacred arrows, each a different color, which also stood for the Cheyenne tribe itself.

A man became a chief by birth or election. He served more as a counselor, an advice giver, than as a commander. His own bravery, above all else, kept him in power. If he should lose his confidence or courage, his people would replace him. A large group (as among the Cheyenne) shared the problems and responsibilities of their people during peace and war.

SOCIAL STANDING

High social standing among the Plains Indians was achieved in a variety of ways. As long as their nomadic life was based on the bison, being a successful hunter was the quickest, surest way to get social standing. With time there was a growing emphasis on warfare as a main way to get honor and importance within the tribe.

Later, the horse raid became equally important as a way to gain standing. A man was judged by the number of horses he had captured. Such a wealthy man was expected to loan horses to poor men. A rich man with a good war record who shared his horses in this way had the chance to become a chief.

SOCIAL GROUPS

Military Groups

A tribe was divided into military groups[5] such as Dog, Fox, Lance, Bowstring,[6] and Shield. When a young man was ready to go on the warpath, he made an effort to join one of these military groups. Shared interests and special war rituals were the basis of each military society.

Each tribe had a society made up of the very bravest of the warriors. The Kaitsenho Society of the Kiowa tribe was such a group; its members carried a crooked lance wrapped with otter's skin. A Kaitsenho Society warrior entered the battle wearing a long buckskin sash around his neck or waist. He would jump off his horse, drive his lance through the sash, and stand pinned to the spot, fighting until he was killed or was freed by one of his friends. He was not allowed to free himself, as the disgrace this action would bring would be worse than death.

Women's Social Groups

Among the Cheyenne there was just one small social group, the Quiller's Society. It was a great honor to be taken into this society, whose members made, or supervised the making of, clothing decorations. This quillwork was actually a ritual, a sacred ceremony.

MARRIAGE CUSTOMS

In some tribes the young girl was guarded until the Maiden Ceremony, which was something like a coming-out party. After this celebration a young woman was considered to be of marriageable age. Hidatsa, Kiowa, and Omaha girls were almost always consulted about the choice of a husband.

A young man had to prove his courage before he could marry. Only after he had taken part in several battles or raids would he have the standing (and later, the horses)[7] to ask a father for a girl of his choice.

Each man who wished to marry chose a bride from outside his clan. (The rule against marriages between clan members or close relatives exists in many cultures.)

An Arapaho or Cheyenne young man might go to live with his wife's parents as a kind of hired hand. A Crow or Blackfeet couple often went to live near, or with, the man's parents.

Many men had more than one wife. If a man died, his widow would become his brother's wife. Often a sister of a man's first wife would become the second wife in a household. Although in some tribes the husband had complete power over the wife, a woman was allowed to leave a mean husband, divorce him, and even remarry.

TRIBAL LAWS AND CUSTOMS

A council of respected elders and warriors usually made the laws and handed out the justice within a tribe. For example, murder was sometimes punished by banishing the guilty one—or the exact punishment could be decided by the relatives of the dead person.

There were, however, some general laws that were shared by most of the Plains tribes. These included:

- You have the responsibility to be kind and respectful—but not groveling—to others. This includes honoring your elders in word and action, not trying to change the way another person believes, not asking personal questions of guests, and not staring at a stranger.

- You should be truthful and honest. Keep every promise you make.

- Always be hospitable, offering food, drink, protection to anyone—even an enemy— while they are in your tipi. When you, on the other hand, are a guest in another's lodge, follow their ways, whatever they may be.

- You should share food with any hungry person in your camp.

- You must be respectful of Mother Nature, never leaving trash behind when you change campsites, never uselessly destroying nature or its beauty.

Tiospaye—this name refers to the extended families within a group or a tribe. Such a distinction is still made and its implied responsibilities are still honored by Sioux today.

Notes for "Social Order and Government"

1. A *tribe* was larger than a band. The members of a tribe lived in the same area, spoke the same language, and shared the same religious beliefs.

2. A *clan* was a family group made up of people who all had an ancestor, real or mythic, in common. Members of a clan were related on the mother's side in some cases, or through the father's side in others, but never through both. In times of need, clan members could be expected to help one another.

3. Families in an area might join together to form a *band.* These groups could have as few as twenty people or as many as three hundred! If the land was rich or had lots of game, the band could be large; if food was hard to get, the band would be small. Most bands chose a very wise or experienced person to be their leader. Some bands had different leaders for different problem areas.

4. Among the Comanches, each band was independent and there was no tribal government. The bands did not fight together on raids as a single force, but neither did they ever fight one another. There were just three kinds of leaders: peace chief, war chief, and band council (and none of these had much true power). It was a loose unity but they were all Comanches, and this gave them great strength against outsiders.

5. The Comanches were an exception. They had no separate military groups.

6. The Bowstrings were also called the Contraries. They were few in number—and very strange, for they did everything backwards. They never married; rather, they lived alone and apart from the village. In battle they would carry their Contrary Bow, which was a lance, and charge the enemy whenever their tribe was retreating. When a Cheyenne had a vision telling him to become a Contrary, it was a burden as well as a sacred responsibility.

7. Among the Cheyenne if a young couple ran off together without making this payment, it was said that the bride had been "stolen."

WAR AND WARRIORS

The early Plains Indians had an unusual way of thinking about war. It was as if each thing a man did in battle was worth a certain number of points. The bigger the risks he took, the bigger the honors (the more points) he earned for himself and his tribe.

It was the earning of war honors—to become known as especially brave and exceptional—that seems to have been the main reason for early warring between Plains people.

A war party would leave their camp on foot, stopping once in a while to smoke or rest. They'd walk quickly, twenty-five miles a day, for some days; but once near their enemy, they would slow down. Each brave wore a bundle on his back that contained: extra moccasins, an awl, sinew for repairs, one or two rawhide ropes for lassoes (if they were on a horse raid), tobacco and a little pipe, and his war medicine. For weapons a man would carry bow and arrows, a very sharp knife, perhaps a gun. Occasionally a wife would also go along, saying: "If my husband were to be killed on this war party, I want to die too."

Taking a scalp meant more than simply killing an enemy[1]; in the end, who won the battle was not so important as how much courage had been shown by each of the warriors in the fighting.

THE COUP

The very greatest honor in war, and so the most points, went to the man who, either unarmed or with his coupstick,[2] succeeded in touching an enemy—man, woman or child. This was called *counting coup*, from the French word for "a blow" or a "strike."[3]

Because of the incredible risk involved, it was much more of a feat and an honor to count coup on an armed enemy than to kill him! The most honor came to a brave who counted coup and captured, at the same time, the enemy's weapons, horse, and ceremonial shield and bag. This brought the warrior large gifts from his people and greater influence.

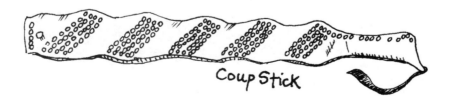

Coup Stick

92

THE SHIELD

Warriors felt that the designs on their war shields, which were received in dreams, protected them in battle. A man waited until he met the enemy before uncovering the shield, and in this way saved up its power until the moment it was needed. These great circles of leather effectively protected the braves against arrows and spears; only when bullets were introduced did they lose their power in battle.

The war shield was the brave's most prized possession and was laid under his head at his death.

So it was that the thrill of the raid, the winning of war honors, and (eventually) the capturing of horses meant so much to some braves that they might make forty or fifty raids before they left the warpath.

Once back at camp, the warriors feasted; a victorious brave would wear his personal war shirt. The deeds of the raid had to be described to the tribal council. If a warrior was found to be truthful and worthy, he was given a coup feather—the tail feather of a male golden eagle, known for its bravery and swiftness. Coup feathers were worn on the bottom of the warrior's scalp-lock; if he collected enough of them, he would wear them on a war bonnet.

FEATHERS

Feathers were worn by warriors to announce their victories and honors. The Dakota Sioux recorded their war feats on eagle feathers in the following ways:

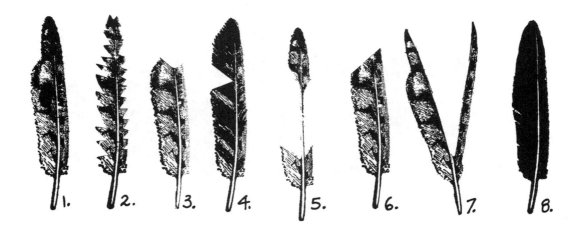

(1) Wearer killed an enemy; *(2)* Wearer counted coup four times; *(3)* Wearer's first coup; *(4)* Wearer cut enemy's throat and took his scalp; *(5)* Wearer counted coup five times; *(6)* Wearer slit enemy's throat; *(7)* Wearer was wounded many times; *(8)* Wearer was wounded in battle.

Most men wore only one or two feathers when they went out on a raid. These were part of their war "medicine" and practical because they were light.

WAR BONNETS

A man had to earn the right to have a feathered war bonnet. He had to win many honors and victories in battle, and then had to collect the eagle feathers needed for the headdress. Finally, it was only with the permission of the other braves that he could wear it.

Photo 20. Mars-Che-Coodo (White Man Runs Him), Crow; 1910. *Photo by DeLancey Gill. Courtesy Museum of New Mexico (neg. no. 59447).*

The one who was to have the war bonnet gathered the main men of his tribe for a feast. After this feast each guest prepared a feather for the bonnet. Then as each feather was handed to the owner, he told of how it had been earned. He, in turn, gave it to the one who was making the headdress and it was put in place. Thirty to fifty feathers went into a war bonnet; and, because each had a story, it might take several weeks to finish one of these head pieces.

The Sioux War Bonnet

The feathers were sewn onto a buckskin skull cap. Then a long strip of buckskin, called a trail, was also sewn to the skullcap. (Before horses, the trails came to the waist; later they were so long that when a brave dismounted, they dragged on the ground.) Sometimes two trails were needed in order to hold all the feathers a man had earned. Once the feathers were in place, the cap was decorated with a band of quill or beadwork. Strips of weasel fur were added—as this animal is clever at escaping hunters and it was thought that this power would then be given to the owner of the bonnet.

The Cheyenne Headdress

In the center of the circle of feathers that formed this bonnet stood a "plume," the peeled shaft of a tall feather to which was tied eagle down. This plume stood for the wearer, and the surrounding feathers were the men he had overcome in battle. Horse hairs tied at each feather's tip stood for the victim's scalp-lock.

Most tribes of the southern and central plains wore the "swept back" type of war bonnet on which the feathers all flowed toward the back.

The Blackfeet War Bonnet

This style had the feathers sewn straight up from a wide headband.

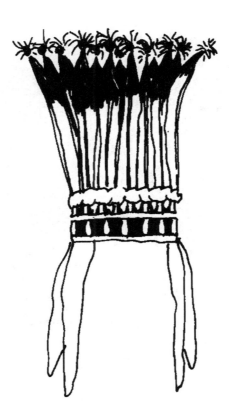

Sometimes a very great warrior or medicine man was given the honor of wearing buffalo horns on his headdress. These horns were hollowed or split to make them light, and then highly polished. Such horns on a war bonnet stood for great strength and personal power.

THE WAR SHIRT

The war shirt was believed to have great medicine, which would protect the wearer; yet, it could only be worn for special occasions and by men who had shown great courage in battle or great wisdom as leaders.

A war shirt was often painted and was heavily beaded or quilled. The Crow and Blackfeet decorated them with weasel fur. The Cheyenne and Dakota war shirts were trimmed with hair, and so were often called "scalp shirts," although this was not always exactly the case. Sometimes the hair was from the brave's own head, or from his wife's, or from the mane or tail of his horse. Each lock of hair on the shirt stood for a coup he had earned.

Usually a war shirt was not worn into battle, but was put on only for the victory celebration.

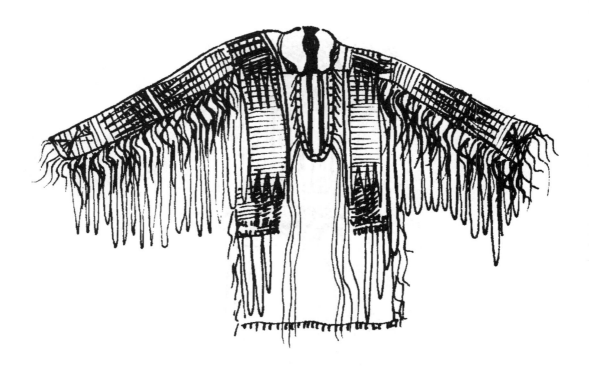

Notes for "War and Warriors"

1. The Piegans, for example, believed that the souls of the enemy killed and scalped were given to their relations in the other world as slaves.

2. Pronounced "coo-stick," this was at first simply a long thin willow stick. As war became more formalized, men made personal coupsticks on which they each kept a record of their accomplishments.

3. Some tribes also counted the capture of an enemy's horse or the touching of his tipi as a coup. Some tribes counted three coup for touching, killing, and then scalping an enemy.

THE HORSE

The horses used by the Native Americans on the Great Plains were descended from Spanish (Andalusian) stallions that Cortéz and his *conquistadores* brought to Mexico. The harsh winter weather in North America coarsened their beauty, perhaps, but it also made them exceedingly strong.

The Sioux first called the horse Shunka WaKan (Mysterious Dog). The Blackfeet called it Elk Dog and the Comanches called it Good Dog. By 1750 wild bands of horses roamed the prairies. These animals—and the rifle—brought about one of the most colorful cultures in human history, that of the buffalo-hunting Plains Indians.

The Plains people got their horses by trading or stealing them from Spanish settlers; or by tracking wild bands of these animals. To capture a wild horse, the Plains Indian tracked it without let-up. When the exhausted animal was forced to rest, the brave went slowly toward it, plaited rope in hand. Swiftly he would throw the lariat over the horse's head. The animal would struggle and kick but finally, nearly strangled, it would grow quiet; then the man would go up to the horse and would breathe gently into its nostrils. Calmed at last, the mustang would be led away by its new master.

HUNTING BUFFALO WITH HORSES

By the middle 1700s tribes such as the Comanches[1] owned large herds of horses, on which they would ride out onto the vast Great Plains in search of buffalo. Now many tribes left their fields and permanent homes to become wanderers again—just like their ancestors, following the herds, staying at night in moveable lodges.

To control his horse in the hunt, the Plains Indian used a simple bridle made of a length of braided leather with two half hitches that were fastened around the lower jaw of the animal. The long ends of the braided strip led back on either side of the animal's neck and these were used as reins.

Each man usually rode a specially trained horse that would bolt away from a wounded bison before the beast could hook it with its horns. Such horses were marked with a notch in the ear to set them apart from the other ponies.

To conduct a good buffalo hunt, the men had to be organized. A brave stripped down to breechcloth and moccasins. From his belt hung a sheath knife. Often he fastened a rawhide thong around his horse's neck so he could grab it and remount quickly if he fell off. A second sinew rope sometimes trailed behind the pony, for the same purpose.

Photo 21. Comanche approaching Colonel Dodge and party between Washita (Wichita) and Red River; by George Catlin; circa 1832–39. *Courtesy Museum of New Mexico (neg. no. 139986).*

To help him stay on his horse in the midst of a thundering bison herd, the rider usually had his knees held down by a leather strap that ran under the horse's belly.

Each hunter held a short lance, or a three-foot bow and twenty iron-tipped arrows, in one hand as he rode, and could shoot the arrows with amazing ease and speed. His target was a spot just behind the last rib of the buffalo—that's where the diaphragm is located. Once the diaphragm was punctured, the bison's lungs would collapse. It usually took three hits to weaken the animal enough for a man to be able to give it the death blow.

One hunting plan the riders used was called "the surround." Two lines, one on either side, closed up the flanks of the herd. As the buffalo began running, the forward riders turned the lead buffalo back into the herd. This caused a swirling chaos of animals and allowed the hunters to ride in and out, shooting and stabbing the woolly beasts. All was confusion now—horses were gored, riders fell and were trampled to death—but the kill was made.

Then the women came on the field. Each identified her husband's arrows and set to work, cutting up and dressing the meat, loading the pack horses.[2]

HOW THE HORSE CHANGED WARRING

Once the Plains Indians began using horses, they would sometimes ride into enemy lands to "make war," but these were most often simply raids by small groups of braves intent on the capture of horses. (Raids like this were sometimes carried out on foot, even after they arrived on the horse.)

Before riding out to do battle, a warrior would paint his horse to show others what victories he had already won. Here are some messages that horses could carry:

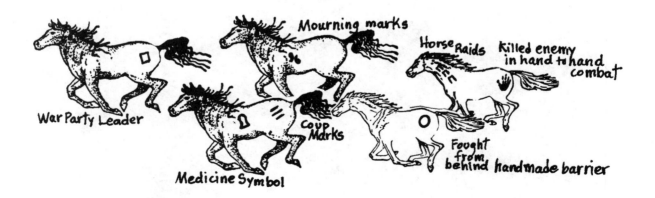

FIREARMS

Firearms, used for hunting and warring, became available to the Plains Indians as soon as they made contact with European traders and trappers.

When a brave set out with the war party, he carried his rifle inside its fringed leather case on his back, with the stock upright. In case of attack he reached back and gripped the stock with his right hand and swiftly pulled the rifle out of its case.

THE SIOUX WAR BONNET

The well-known Sioux war bonnet was actually made possible by the horse! This headdress was so large and awkward that it could only be worn by a man on horseback. Matched eagle plumes, each standing for a special deed, were loosely fastened to a cap that was bordered by a decorative headband. Ermine tails hung down on either side of the headband. These bonnets had either one or two long feather trailers.

THE NEW LIFE ON THE PLAINS

The horse changed may things for the Plains people. With the horse the people could move around more easily and were able to carry bigger tipis and more possessions.[3] Both wars and hunting were sped up. It became easier to trade with tribes from much farther away.

Photo 22. Piegan with a travois; circa 1907. *Courtesy Museum of New Mexico (neg. no. 88707).*

Horses were thought to be sacred gifts from the gods and were treated respectfully. Soon they became the sign of wealth and power. When a young man wished to marry, he often could persuade his future father-in-law (as well as the bride-to-be) by the number and quality of the horses he offered.

Yet the arrival of the horse also brought some problems: the balance between the tribes was upset. Those nations with the most horses became the richest, the strongest, the most envied.

Now the Plains woman, who had shared the life of the Plains man, was more often left at the campsite while the men on horseback rode off to raid, war, trade, or hunt. It became more difficult for the women to keep up with the large number of hides the men gave them. Soon the best hunters began taking second wives to help with the work and this also made village life different.

Gradually, other tribes from the east, forced out by European-American settlers, began arriving on the Great Plains. These new groups collected horses, organized bison hunts, and took part in the new life of the Plains. With time these different tribes and their customs blended into a great new culture—filled with ceremonies, dances, extraordinary costumes, horsemanship, bravery in battle—shaped and made possible by the coming of the horse.

Notes for "The Horse"

1. The Apaches were an exception; they never became really involved in horse-owning and riding. Because they lived in dry and rugged surroundings, there was little enough food for the people, let alone for livestock. The Apache traveled this harsh land on foot, catching and gathering food as they went. Actually, most of the time, that's how the Apache looked at the horse—worth more as *food* than as *transportation.*

2. Buffalo hearts were left on the plains as offerings, to make certain that there would be young buffalo born to replace the dead.

3. The sledge, or travois, that had carried goods, children, the sick and the old had always been drawn by village dogs. Now the bigger, stronger horse was harnessed to the travois, pulling much heavier, larger loads.

THE EUROPEANS COME

Plains Indian life was extraordinary and yet its Golden Age lasted only a little more than a century. The Europeans' horse made that life possible, and the advance of the white man brought that way of life to a terrible end.

By the mid-1700s some Europeans, mostly French and English traders, had reached the eastern edges of the Great Plains. They were hunting beaver for their skins, which were taken back to Europe to be made into fur hats. Then in 1804-1806 The Lewis and Clark Expedition passed through, and their reports of the great beauty and wealth they saw made many European people become interested in moving west.

The early pioneers did not, at first, try to settle in the Great Plains, because the weather was harsh all year long and the earth was hard-packed and difficult to farm.

Early on (and up to about 1840) the meetings and dealings between the Plains tribes and the white men were generally friendly; but things were changing. With the killing of both beaver and buffalo, brought about by the demands of the fur trade, and with the increased flow into and across the Plains of pioneers, settlers, and then gold miners, the good feelings between the natives and the whites began to disappear.

Hundreds of traders and trappers came up the Missouri River from 1808 on. With them came trading posts, liquor, and eventually a dependence on white men's guns, blankets, iron kettles, glass beads, and bolts of cloth.

CHANGES IN EVERYDAY LIFE

The coming of the Europeans brought about changes in the day-to-day life of the Plains people.

Food

The native people learned to bake wheat bread in Dutch ovens, and they prepared coffee by smashing the beans with an ax handle and then boiling the powder in water. (See Photo 23.)

Buffalo Bird Woman recalled, "I was not quite 20 (in about 1855) when we bought an iron pot for cooking. Before that we used only earthen pots for cooking in our family."

Photo 23. Sioux camp 101, Ranch Show, Jamestown (Virginia) Exposition; 1907. *Photo by Keystone View Co. Courtesy Museum of New Mexico (neg. no. 90012).*

Clothing

Once trade with the Europeans became popular, belts were decorated with small brass tacks (Northern Plains), beads, silver, or German silver conchos (Central and Southern Plains).

Photo 24. Unidentified woman. *Photo by E. B. Snell. Courtesy Museum of New Mexico (neg. no. 150097).*

Bolts of calico cloth were an important trade item and the Plains people enjoyed using this new material for dresses and shawls. Warm woven blankets were also favored.

The vest seems to be a piece of clothing the Native Americans adopted from the Europeans.

Shelter

As canvas became available in the late 1800s, the design and construction of tipis changed and regional variations developed.

Photo 25. Apache camp: circa 1935. Photo by T. Harmon Parkhurst. Courtesy Museum of New Mexico (neg. no. 2077).

Tipi poles in the north lifted higher above the smoke hole than they did on the southern Plains and often colorful flags or trophy scalps could be seen tied to these taller poles.

Tools

Bone, wooden, and stone tools were replaced by metal knives, hoes, shovels, and so on.

Photo 26. Pawnee man; circa 1868–70. *Photo by Jackson Brothers. Courtesy Museum of New Mexico (neg. no. 139525).*

FIREARMS AND WARRING TOOLS

With the gun and rifle came the new accessories—the powder horn and ammunition. The European rifle became the basis for the design of a new war club, called the gunstock club. It was often decorated with brass tacks, another European trade item.

Photo 27. Kiowa Chief Poor Buffalo. *Photo by Carson Brothers. Courtesy Museum of New Mexico (neg. no. 144747).*

Photo 28. Ojibwa "Arrowmaker." *Courtesy Museum of New Mexico (neg. no. 41745).*

Arts and Crafts

PAINT PIGMENTS

After the 16th century, brilliant pigments were available through trade with the Europeans; these paints were used on clothing as well as tipis and tipi liners.

GLASS BEADS

Most of these beads were handmade in Venice. Native Americans enthusiastically traded their fur pelts for the bright, sturdy and plentiful new craft material. Soon glass beads took the place of handmade (shell, bone and clay) beads and quillwork.

The native people adapted these European beads to their own crafts in unique ways. Their small round shape allowed the beadworker to make curves and circles in her designs, which the flat straight-sided quills had never allowed.

In a short time Native American women brought the craft of beadwork to new levels of design perfection.

These necklaces, which were rare and precious before the coming of the Europeans, became more common after a man in Illinois found a way to mass produce them from the legs of slaughtered cattle.

MAJOR CONSEQUENCES

The traders also, unknowingly, brought with them hideous diseases—smallpox, measles, diphtheria—against which the Native people had no defense; they died by the thousands.[1]

The use of guns quickly made some tribes stronger than others, breaking down the general equality[2] among them that had been true for the previous hundred years.

The Great Plains were huge but, eventually, even they were not big enough for the native Plains people and the pioneers flooding in from the East. The U.S. Government encouraged, bribed and, sometimes, forced the Plains Indians to sign legal agreements, some of which they did not even understand. The Plains tribes were made to get off some of the land in exchange for promises that they could keep the rest. From the time of 1850 on, there were misunderstandings, anger, endless broken promises—and massacres and counter-slaughters of both the Plains people and the whites.

Broken Treaties and the American Indian Wars

Between 1865-1890 there were a dozen campaigns and almost 1,000 engagements between the Plains Indians and the U.S. Army. Here is a partial list of major clashes:

1835	Texas Rangers campaign against Comanches
1854	The Gratton Affair in Wyoming: Sioux
1857	Battle of Solomon Fork in Kansas: Cheyenne
1862-3	Santee Sioux uprising in Minnesota, under Chief Little Crow
1863	The Shoshoni War (Bear River Campaign) in Utah and Idaho
1863-4	Santee Sioux and Teton Sioux uprising in North Dakota
1864	Sandcreek Massacre: Chivington's Colorado Volunteers kill over 300 Native Americans
1864-5	Cheyenne-Arapaho War in Colorado and Kansas
1866-8	War for Bozeman Trail, in Wyoming and Montana: Cheyenne and Arapaho, under Chief Red Cloud
1867	Hancock Campaign in Central Plains, against Cheyenne and Arapaho
1868-9	Southern Plains War (Sheridan Campaign): Cheyenne, Arapaho, Sioux, Kiowa, and Comanches

1874-5	Red River War in Southern Plains: Comanche, Kiowas, and Cheyennes, under Quanah Parker
1876-7	Sioux War for the Black Hills: Sioux, Cheyenne, and Arapaho, under the command of Crazy Horse and Sitting Bull
1876	Battle of Little Big Horn
1879	Ute War in Colorado
1890	Battle at Wounded Knee on the Rosebud Reservation: 350 Sioux massacred by U.S. troops. Considered to be the end of the American Indian Wars.

The story of these wars differ a lot depending on who is telling it. Of course, this is true of all history. But there is one thing on which both sides agree: in the beginning the Plains people had the land and they wanted to keep it and they wanted to go on living their lives there, free to hunt buffalo and to roam wherever they liked.[3]

For 130 years the killing and counter-killing went on. The whites saw the Plains people as uncivilized, uneducated, and lacking good sense. The native people saw the whites as endlessly greedy, untrustworthy, and an enemy to their way of life.

It was natural that the native people would fight to protect what they had. And they did fight, fiercely and bravely. Some of these battles are now legendary: The Battle of Little Big Horn, the Massacre at Wounded Knee, and the names of the great war leaders, Sitting Bull, Red Cloud, Crazy Horse, and Quanah Parker live on. Both sides did cruel things during these wars, such as killing the unarmed and scalping the dead. Both sides lost many courageous men.

Time and again the U.S. leaders from the east met with Native American peace parties and signed treaties that "allowed" the Plains people to keep certain lands for their own. Then, after a while, white settlers would need these lands on which to spread out and develop farms, railroads, mines, stores, and towns—so "civilization" might come to this "new" land. The treaties would be broken and the tribes would be forced onto even smaller lands.

This was the case in the Black Hills in the western part of present-day South Dakota. This rugged land was not fit for farming, so the Dakota Sioux were promised they might keep these hills, which are sacred to them. The treaty of 1868 promised peace for "as long as the grass shall grow and the rivers flow." Two months later the U.S. Government, realizing that the Black Hills' gold was more valuable than any treaty, sent a new agreement to the Sioux with a warning: Sign or Starve to Death.

In the end it was not the army soldiers, the huge numbers of repeating rifles, nor the forts and cannon that defeated the Plains Indians. Rather, it was the killing of all the buffalo that would end their way of life! By the fall of 1873 the plains were whitened with bleaching buffalo bones.[4]

The Buffalo Is Gone

In 1800 there were an estimated sixty million buffalo on the Plains. In the years when the pioneers were moving westward, there were so many bison that sometimes a herd would stop a riverboat midstream, or block—and even derail—a train crossing the prairies.

Military officers and government officials decided that the Indians could be weakened by purposely cutting off their main food supply. The herds of buffalo didn't stand a chance.

The organized slaughter of the herds began in 1870 when the railroads were being built. Rather than bring in food for the railroad workers, the managers hired professional riflemen to kill the buffalo. Only "the choice pieces," the tongue and the hump, were cut out of the animals, and the prairies were littered with thousands of rotting carcasses.

Once the railroad lines had been completed, it became a popular "sport" to ride slowly along and, from the safety of a railroad car, shoot at the milling bison herds. As each train passed on, it left the prairie covered with dead animals—"A uniquely American scene" one British traveler wrote back to England.

Then buffalo hunting became organized to provide skins for tanners in the East, who paid three dollars a piece for each hide; one single hunter working with a team of skinners claimed he could kill 1,500 bison in a week!

The U.S. Government wanted the Native Americans to accept the new situation, to become farmers and herdsmen in the European way. The warring continued and many brave men and defenseless women and children were killed; by 1881 hardly a tribesman was left roaming free on the Great Plains. And, by the end of the century, only a thousand buffalo were left alive.

Tribe after tribe began to starve—often they were forced to live on reservations that were filthy and poor. The Golden Age of the Plains people was at an end.

Photo 29. Sioux (?) men; 1890. *Photo by J. C. H. Grabill. Courtesy Museum of New Mexico (neg. no. 77783).*

Resettlement

Now came the period when the Plains Indians were relocated to various reservations, many of these far away from their homelands. (See **The Plains Indians Today** and the reproducible maps.)

Religion

The white men believed that it was their responsibility to convert the Plains Indians to Christianity. They tried to do this by forbidding native rituals such as the widely practiced Sun Gaze Dance[5] (described in the **Religion** section) and by preaching the benefits of their own religion and way of life.

From the earliest period of contact most tribal leaders urged their people to not get used to European goods—especially alcohol—and to stay in touch with their tribal way of living. Many of these leaders foretold the future—how land would be lost, how wars would follow, and the buffalo would disappear. Because of such predictions, these early leaders were sometimes called prophets by the Europeans.

Photo 30. Piegan Offerings in a Sun Lodge; 1926. *Photo by Edward S. Curtis. Courtesy Museum of New Mexico (neg. no. 143857).*

In the 1880s Wovoka, a Paiute prophet, had a vision during an eclipse of the sun. In the vision he was told to spread the teachings of his father, Tavibo. These teachings came to be known as the Ghost Dance religion.[6]

In 1889 it spread quickly throughout the defeated and desperate nations of the Plains. The Ghost Dance religion promised that if the Native Americans practiced its rites, the present world of white intruders and destroyers would disappear. It would be replaced with a wild and beautiful land, filled with buffalo.

In spite of the fervent prayers, dancing, and the heartfelt trust placed in it, the Ghost Dance religion proved to be a horrible disaster. In 1890, with the massacre of its believers by the U.S. Army, this religion came to an end.

Then, at the turn of the 20th century, Quanah Parker, the last great American Indian prophet, learned of the Peyote Road. He helped to found the Native American Church, which spread to the Plains and the prairies, and is still practiced today. It offers a variation of Christianity at the same time that it preserves some of the native ways and beliefs. For example, sweat baths are used for cleansing and peyote is used as a means to gain visions. (The use of peyote is illegal in some places and the Native American Church has been involved in legal battles, claiming their right to use it is protected by the Freedom of Religion section of the U.S. Constitution.)

Photo 31. Unidentified Plains Men. *Photo by Soule & Burkhart. Courtesy Museum of New Mexico (neg. no. 58618).*

Education

As early as the 1830s missionaries and well-wishers tried to educate the Plains Indian children in white ways. By the 1870s "Indian Schools" were being founded with the idea of blending tribal peoples into the white culture. Often after their resettlement on reservations, young boys and girls were taken to boarding schools far from their tribes and families. The result of these efforts to educate and "to civilize" Plains tribe children was that whole generations of youngsters had their birthrights removed. After being educated in white schools with white values, many of the young people tried to return to the reservations, only to see that they no longer were truly Plains Indians—nor were they white. The graduates of these schools were now displaced persons.

Photo 32. Ruth (daughter of Big Head), Hattie (daughter of Lone Wolf), Anna Laura (daughter of Shooting Cat), Grace (daughter of Cook), and Stella (daughter of Chasing Hawk); Sioux students at Training School in Carlisle, Pennsylvania; circa 1880. *Photo by John N. Choate. Courtesy Museum of New Mexico (neg. no. 87563).*

Photo 33. Reuben (son of Quick Bear), Bernard (son of Ring Thunder), John Renville (son of Gabriel Renville), Horace (son of Coarse Voice), and Rufus (son of Black Crow); Sioux students at Training School in Carlisle, Pennsylvania; circa 1880. *Photo by John N. Choate. Courtesy Museum of New Mexico (neg. no. 87565).*

Notes for "The Europeans Come"

1. The Mandan and Arikara were among the tribes that had the most contact with the whites. In the early 1800s epidemics reduced the Mandans from 3,600 to just 125 by 1837.

2. The Shoshoni had a hard time getting guns because the Spanish, with whom they traded in New Mexico, would not sell firearms to native people. As chief Cameahwait told Lewis and Clark: "But this should not be . . . . If we had guns, instead of hiding ourselves in the mountains and living like bears on roots and berries, we would then go down and live in buffalo country in spite of our enemies, whom we never fear when we meet on equal terms."

3. In about 1860 Samuel N. Latta, Indian Agent for the Upper Missouri area, described the Plains tribesmen he met: "A powerful and warlike people, proud, haughty, and defiant. Well over six feet in height, strong muscular frames and very good horsemen, well dressed, principally in skins and robes; rich in horses and lodges; have a great abundance of meat since buffalo, elk, antelope and deer abound in their country. They say they are Indians and do not wish to change their mode of living."

4. Sitting Bull, the Sioux medicine man (see **Famous Native Americans**), was quoted in *The New York Herald* of November 16, 1877, as saying: "We kill buffaloes, as we kill other animals, for food and clothing. They [the Americans] kill buffaloes—for what? Go through [the] country. See the thousands of carcasses rotting on the Plains. Your young men shoot for pleasure. All they take from the dead buffalo is his tail, or his head, or his horns, perhaps, to show they have killed a buffalo. What is this? Is it robbery? You call us savages. What are they?"

5. Parts of the Sun Dance were outlawed by the U.S. Government in the 1880s. This was done to try and break up the native religion of the Plains people—and also because many settlers were revolted by the torture of the Sun Dance traditions.

    The Comanches only practiced the Sun Dance on one occasion, in about 1873, when they were on particularly hard times. The prophet Ishatai convinced them that if they held a Sun Dance, they would gain favor with the Great Spirit and would be protected from white men's bullets; then, when the Europeans were gone, the buffalo would return! The Comanches performed the ritual and then rode against Adobe Walls, a small hunters' outpost. The white hunters, with their powerful and accurate buffalo rifles, slaughtered much of the war party, which was forced to retreat. The Comanches never performed the Sun Dance again.

6. The most important item of this religion was the Ghost Dance Shirt. Black Elk, a young Sioux, had a vision in which the Great Spirit gave him the ghost shirt that had the wonderful power to ward off white men's bullets and weapons. During the dance the shirt was worn on the outside and at all other times it was worn as an inner garment.

As animal skins were scarce by 1890, some ghost shirts were made of unbleached muslin. Every shirt was alike in its shape, fringe, eagle feathers, and sinew-sewn seams. The painting varied from very simple to complex designs of the heavens and Plains mythology. Red paint on the shirt or fringe stood for the Messiah.

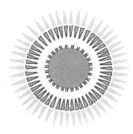

THE PLAINS INDIANS TODAY

Where are those tribal people of the Great Plains and the Prairies today? How do the great-great-grandchildren of the Plains warriors clothe and house themselves in the 20th century? What part of their ancestors' lives still influence these people today?

POPULATION

The 1990 Census tells us that there are about 1,800,000 Native Americans living in the United States today. About 400,000 (23%) live on reservations[1] and 1,400,000 (77%) live in cities[2] and suburban areas.

The American Indian population in the present-day states of the Plains is as follows, according to the 1990 census:

State	Native American Population of State	% of Total Population of the State
Oklahoma	252,420	8.0%
Texas	65,877	0.4%
South Dakota	50,575	7.3%
Minnesota	49,909	1.1%
Montana	47,679	6.0%
North Dakota	25,917	4.1%
Kansas	21,965	0.9%
Illinois	21,836	0.2%
Missouri	19,835	0.4%
Idaho	13,780	1.4%
Nebraska	12,410	0.8%
Wyoming	9,479	2.1%
Iowa	7,390	0.3%

THE RESERVATIONS

Four of the largest reservations in the U.S., by population, are located in the Great Plains area: Pine Ridge, South Dakota (pop. 12,113); Fort Apache, South Dakota (pop. 10,394); Rosebud, South Dakota (pop. 9,696); and Blackfeet Reservation, Montana (pop. 8,549).

American Indians born on reservations usually stay on the reservations; although they may leave sometimes, they often return. When an American Indian is born off the reservation, there is only a remote chance that he or she will go live on a reservation later in life. The most recent census figures show there are today more native people living in urban settings than in rural ones.

As a general rule only American Indians living on a reservation get U.S. Government help in the form of housing, utilities, health care, and educational aid.

Finding a stable source of income on a reservation has always been difficult. The number of businesses located on the reservations and owned by Native Americans grew in the 1980s; there was growth in construction companies, car sales, food and goods stores, farming, and trucking.

Most native people today live in two worlds; many want to continue their traditions and their cultural ties, while at the same time work (and live) in the modern world. Even traditional people living on reservations have adapted to parts of 20th-century white culture and values. Televisions, telephones, modern clothing, modern housing, cars—have all made their appearance on the reservations.

Nevertheless, Native Americans continue to face harsh problems on and off the reservation.

PROBLEMS: EMPLOYMENT, EDUCATION, HEALTH

Jobs and Income

Almost one half of all Native Americans are out of work; of those *with* jobs, three quarters earn less than $7,000 a year. (The average household income in the U.S. in 1992 was $30,786.)

Many tribal leaders believe that only jobs can solve the serious problems of poverty and alcoholism on and off the reservations.

GAMING ON INDIAN LANDS

In recent years high-stake bingo and gambling casinos have become a way for tribes to make money and bring jobs to the reservation. Because these operations are on American Indian land, where local and state laws don't apply, they can offer activities not allowed off-reservation. Their federal tax-exempt status gives Native Americans a definite advantage over other gambling establishments in so far as gambling receipts are concerned. Often the profits are used to fund health clinics, to offer housing for the elderly, and to build classrooms for the reservation schools.

There are questions concerning the casinos: how should the profits be shared? Should the U.S. Government continue to give the same (health, education, housing) services to people who may now be wealthy? Should the casinos give a percentage to the Native American housing and educational services located in cities where their tribal people work and live? These are not simple questions and each tribe must find its own answers.

Education

Just about half (52%) of all Native Americans finish high school; about 20% go to college and, of these, only four out of every hundred graduate.

Many Native Americans feel that the best way to improve the lives of their people is through education:

"Today the Native Americans must get ready to take control of their lives: this can be done through education." "The next battles will be won by warriors whose weapons are the briefcase and the computer."[3]

Health

One hundred years ago, the Plains people were attacked and killed by smallpox, measles and diphtheria, diseases brought to this continent by the Europeans. Present-day Native Americans continue to be challenged by serious health problems. Among the native people, the death rate due to drinking alcohol is ten times higher than that of all other races combined. Tuberculosis is seven and a half times more frequent among Native Americans than it is among non-American Indians, and diabetes affects them seven times more than it does the rest of the population.

LANGUAGE

It is estimated that about one third of all Native Americans still speak their tribal language. Among the Plains people, the Apache and the Sioux show the highest percentage of current native language usage.

In the 1980s, on some reservations, Plains people were working fast and hard to video-tape and record elders speaking their unwritten language. Mandan, for example, was spoken by just six people in 1991; in the same year, only five people still spoke the Osage language.

The use of native languages was once forbidden in U.S. schools. In 1990 The Native American Language Act was signed into law by President Bush; it states that it is U.S. policy to "preserve, protect and promote the rights and freedom of Native Americans to use, practice and develop Native American languages."

Storytelling by the elders continues (see "Storytelling" in **Language**). Today, when children spend so much time watching television and videos, we can only wonder if retelling the old stories can compete with the dazzle of the media.

"Perhaps we need not be concerned about all this, but instead should be grateful for the phenomena taking place on most northern plains reservations. Here we see a cultural renaissance of native languages, music and dance, traditional and contemporary visual arts, ethno-history projects from the point of view of natives as researched and written by natives, and the growing participation on all levels of native society in the sacred traditions."

—**Arthur Amiotte, Lakota artist and writer,**
   <u>The Call to Remember</u>[4]

CRAFTS

In the 1950s quillwork was a dying art. But, as Native American studies and a pride in early art forms have increased, more quillwork is being done each year, particularly by the Sioux women.

Bead work and basketry are still done by Plains women and several Native American Art Institutes (including the IAIA [Institute of American Indian Art] in Santa Fe, New Mexico) train young students in the traditional crafts of their ancestors, as well as encouraging them toward individual expression in the arts.

THREATS TO TRADITION

Some traditional Native American sacred practices (ceremonies, prayers, vision quests) must take place at sacred sites that have not been changed by logging, mining, roads, dams, fences, tourists, or electric plants. There are sacred lands which have been kept safe, or have been returned to the tribes; in other cases, such sacred lands have been destroyed.

Medicine Wheel, Wyoming

This is the place in the Big Horn Mountains that is sacred to Blackfeet, Crow, Cheyenne, Lakota, Shoshoni, and Arapaho Indians. In 1991 the U.S. Forest Service made a proposal to develop Medicine Wheel into a tourist destination and to promote logging activities around the area in which this prehistoric "wheel" is located.

Badger Two Medicine, Montana

This site borders the Blackfeet Reservation and is in Lewis and Clark National Forest. It is sacred to Blackfeet and other tribes. It is threatened by oil and gas companies that want to drill there and explore for resources.

Kootenai Falls, Montana

These falls are sacred to native people of Montana, Idaho, and British Columbia. In 1987 this site was saved by a Federal Energy Regulatory Commission ruling that prevented seven Montana-Idaho electric cooperatives from building a dam and power plant at Kootenai Falls. So this sacred site *has* been preserved!

SUMMING UP

The Native Americans are a sturdy and inventive people. They have lived through a 400-year struggle with the Europeans, during which their very existence was at stake. They have lived through one hundred years of BIA and U.S. Government control. Yet they survive. They have strong ties to the earth and to nature, and these have given them strength over the years.

Today, with a population of more than a million and with an annual birth rate twice that of the general population, the first Americans seem to be in no danger of disappearing!

Photo 34. Gros Ventre Chief Red Whip; 1913. *Photo by Joseph A. Dixon. Courtesy Museum of New Mexico (neg. no. 68011).*

Notes for "The Plains Indians Today"

1. The Secretary of the Interior is the main overseer (trustee) for the United States government, and the Bureau of Indian Affairs (BIA) answers to him as it manages these lands. A few reservations are nearly all tribal lands, and others are almost completely owned by private individuals.

2. Because census-takers have had different ways of judging who is an American Indian, it is not easy to know exactly how many live in the larger cities. In any case, we do know that the numbers are rising:

1940	about 5% lived in cities
1950	almost 20% lived in cities
1960	almost 30% lived in cities
1970	44.5% lived in cities
1980	49% lived in cities
1990	51% lived in large cities

3. Now Native Americans can keep in touch and find out what is going on with other native groups by joining computer networks such as Indian Net, Native Net, Aises Net. The quotes in the text, and some of the statistics in this chapter, are from *American Indian Digest, 1995 edition*, by George Russell, a member of the Saginaw Chippewa tribe. To order this book or American Indian history maps, call Thunderbird Enterprises at 1-800-835-7220.

4. *Parabola*, vol. XVII, no. 3, Aug. 1992, pages 29-34.

HISTORIC NATIVE AMERICANS OF THE PLAINS AND PRAIRIES

SITTING BULL, MEDICINE MAN AND SIOUX LEADER

Born in about 1831 in what is today South Dakota, Sitting Bull was fourteen when he went with a war party against the Crow and counted his first coup.[1] This great feat earned him his adult name, Sitting Bull.

He always believed that he was chosen by the Great Spirit to protect and lead his people. Although, while in his thirties, he was lamed by a Crow bullet, he was on the warpath almost continuously from 1866–1881. Other northern Plains tribes might retreat to the reservations, but Sitting Bull and his people would not!

By the spring of 1876, about 3,000 warriors—Teton and Oglala Sioux, Northern Cheyenne, and some Arapaho—had joined Sitting Bull's forces at their camp in the valley of the Little Big Horn River.[2] There they chose Sitting Bull to lead them against the U.S. Government forces.

Sitting Bull was a remarkable leader. He understood that the upcoming battle would be for his people's very existence. That June in 1876, he announced that he would perform the Sun Dance in order to receive a vision of what was to happen for his people. He had often performed this most important and sacred ceremony; the overlapping scars on his chest and back gave witness to the tortures he had gone through.

For this great Sun Dance, Sitting Bull gave 100 pieces of flesh from his arms and shoulders. Then, bleeding heavily, he danced all day and all that night. Around noon of the next day, he lost consciousness and received his vision: There would be many white soldiers upside down, as though falling from the sky, and the Great Spirit would bring the Sioux and Cheyenne to victory.[3] His followers so trusted this sign that they believed beyond a doubt that they would win.

On June 16 Crazy Horse led 1,000 braves against General Crook and his 1,300 armed soldiers at the Battle of the Rosebud. Sitting Bull, weakened by the ordeal of the Sun Dance, was there nonetheless, urging on his warriors. At the day's end, Crook retreated with heavy losses.

A week later, on June 25, 1876, Colonel Custer—who had been a hero in the Civil War—decided to attack the Sioux and Cheyenne camp. His friendly Plains Indian scouts advised him not to, but he was determined to gain fame as "the man who destroyed the Sioux nation." At this time few whites realized the size of the force—about 6,000 men—that was gathered at this place, but the Indians' fighting ability *was* well known. As General Frederick Benteen said, "The Sioux are good shots, good riders and the best fighters the sun ever shone on."

Custer led his 7th Cavalry into a trap and he, and every one of his 224 soldiers, were killed. This battle is named "Custer's Last Stand" or "The Battle of Little Big Horn," for the place in Montana where it was fought. This was the Plains Indians' greatest and last victory; from then on the tribes would all be hunted down, destroyed, or led off to internment camps called reservations.

For some years Sitting Bull and his people wandered in Canada, but in 1881, when the supply of buffalo ran out, they were forced to return to the U.S. and surrender. For two years the Sioux leader was a prisoner of war. He had become so famous that he received hundreds of letters from admirers. In 1883 he was moved to Standing Rock Reservation. Because of his fame, and because Sitting Bull still considered himself the leader of his people, he aroused the anger and jealousy of the reservation agent, James McLaughlin.

In 1885 Sitting Bull toured the world for a year with Buffalo Bill's Wild West Show, but when he returned he was again at odds with Agent McLaughlin. In 1890 he applied for a pass to visit Pine Ridge—a Ghost Dance was to be held there—but he was detained on orders from the agent, who claimed that the elderly medicine man "was planning to escape." On December 15 McLaughlin sent Indian police to seize Sitting Bull, whose friends and family tried to prevent the arrest. During the struggle Sitting Bull, his seventeen-year-old son, and six others were killed.

In 1953, sixty-three years after his death, the remains of this extraordinary man were transferred to Mobridge, South Dakota, where, today, a granite shaft marks the grave of the great leader of the Sioux.

In one of his visions Sitting Bull was warned by a yellow hammer bird that he would soon be attacked by a grizzly bear. The great medicine man was so grateful that he wrote this poem to honor the songbird.

Pretty bird, you saw me and took pity on me;
You wished me to survive among the people.
O Bird People, from this day you shall be my relatives![4]

QUANAH PARKER, COMANCHE WARRIOR AND PEACEMAKER

For many years the word *Comanche* brought terror to Texas settlers. In the early 1800s the Comanches had befriended Europeans and Americans; but they could only be bitter enemies of the Texans who settled in the best of their buffalo-hunting grounds.

On one of their raids on a small settlement in east Texas, in 1835, the Comanches carried away a ten-year-old girl, Cynthia Ann Parker. She grew up to marry the Comanche chief, Nokoni. Their first son, who was born in about 1845, was Quanah Parker. In accordance with Comanche tradition, the baby was given his mother's last name.

Quanah grew to be a talented, intelligent man, a chief himself. In 1867 the U.S. Medicine Lodge Treaty assigned Comanches, Kiowas, Cheyennes, and Arapahoes to reservations, but Chief Parker and his band refused to sign the treaty, continuing to hunt buffalo and attack settlements on the Texas border.

In the early 1870s commercial hunters illegally invaded tribal lands, slaughtering huge numbers of buffalo for their hides, and leaving the meat to rot in the sun. Chief Parker was outraged and, in June 1874, he led 700 warriors—Cheyennes, Kiowas, as well as Comanches—against the post at Adobe Walls, where thirty of the buffalo hunters were staying. For three days Quanah's warriors fought bravely, but the fort was well protected and the men there were well armed. In the end Quanah and his men withdrew. He and his band stayed in the plains until the next summer, when he at last surrendered. He made up his mind then to change, so that he would be able to get along peacefully with the U.S. government. "I can learn the white man's ways," he said. This man who had *never* signed a treaty, now—on his surrender—did so.

He convinced even the wildest of the Comanche bands to come live on the reservations, and only then did peace come to the Texas plains.

For the next thirty years he was the leader of a confederation of Plains tribes. He encouraged them to build homes, plant crops, and formally educate their children. It was his idea to lease out extra pasture lands in order to make money for his people. Although he was modern in many ways, Quanah always practiced the important Indian ceremonies and never gave up his Native American religious beliefs.

Quanah Parker spoke both English and Spanish fluently. He saw to it that all of his many children were well educated. Often he traveled to Washington D.C. to speak with the leaders there on behalf of his people.

He died in 1911, a very esteemed and respected man. In 1957 he was given a new burial, with all military honors, at Fort Sill in Oklahoma.

SUSAN LaFLESCHE PICOTTE, NATIVE AMERICAN DOCTOR

The buffalo were disappearing. It was a time of change for the Plains people when Susan LaFlesche was born in 1865. Her parents believed that if the Omaha tribe was to survive, they would have to become more like the Europeans. Susan grew up to believe this too, and she spent her life helping her people make this change.

Susan first went to a Presbyterian mission school where she and the other children were not allowed to speak their Omaha language. They had to wear strange clothes—uniforms—

and eat foods that were different from their comforting homemade dishes. At night they lay in big silent rooms on flat metal beds; it was not an easy childhood. But Susan made up her mind to do well in her studies and she did, finishing high school and earning a scholarship to Hampton Institute, a school that had originally been opened to educate newly freed African Americans. She graduated from there as class salutatorian.

Susan knew she wanted to be a doctor, but where could she possibly find the money for the tuition? A group of women from the Connecticut Indian Association heard about Susan. They believed in her intelligence and desire to serve her people. They paid for Susan's medical training. On the day of her graduation, Dr. LaFlesche became the very first Native American woman to become a medical doctor.

Once she had her degree, Dr. LaFlesche went back to the Omaha reservation, where she worked among her people healing, teaching, and making them more aware of their legal and human rights. For thirty years she helped the Omaha people, until, in 1915, at the age of fifty, she died. Dr. Susan LaFlesche spent her life trying to improve herself and helping the Omahas all to have better lives.[5]

When the Europeans came to North America, the Cherokees were a great nation. They were helpful in every way to the newcomers. But in the end the white people were cruel to them. In 1838 the Cherokees were forced to leave their homes in the east because their lands were now being taken over by white settlers. The U.S. president, Andrew Jackson, made the Cherokees walk 1,200 miles to an Indian Territory where they were supposed to go and live. There were 16,000 Cherokees when they started that horribly long walk and more than 4,000 of them died on the way. So even today it is called The Trail of Tears.

One hundred years passed and then in 1946 the U.S. government let the Cherokee Nation reorganize. It wasn't until 1971 that the BIA allowed the Cherokees to elect their own chief! And *this* is where Wilma Mankiller comes in!

WILMA MANKILLER, CHIEF OF THE CHEROKEE NATION

Born in an Indian Hospital in Oklahoma, Wilma and her ten brothers and sisters grew up on a farm that had no electricity and no running water! It wasn't an easy life but it was a happy one. They drank the fresh water from the spring and ate the food that they raised and they felt it was good to live in the country.

Then the weather changed and there was no rain at all. The plants died, the crops dried up, and Wilma's family couldn't make a living on the farm anymore.

The U.S. Government tried to help. The Bureau of Indian Affairs paid to move Wilma and her family to San Francisco, California, where there were better opportunities for jobs and a new life. Wilma was twelve years old when they made this move, and it was very hard for her family; living in a big city, trying to make enough money to raise eleven children— and it was lonely to have left their Indian friends back in Oklahoma.

Wilma became a teenager, went to high school, and then to college at San Francisco State University, where she fell in love and eventually married. She and her husband had two little girls who were three and five when Wilma began working to help other American Indian people. She helped raise money. She brought attention to the needs of the Native Americans. Wilma Mankiller became "an activist for Indian rights"!

She was working hard for the American Indians, but life in the city had made her tired. Her marriage wasn't going well any more, so Wilma took her two daughters and went back to Oklahoma. Her father had died and was buried there, and her mother and sisters were all moving back too. Once her children were settled and in school, Wilma began working in the offices of the Cherokee Nation of Oklahoma. She saw how the Native Americans who lived out in the country *still* needed running water and better houses. So she began teaching people how to build and fix up their own houses. She taught them how to put in plumbing, too.

Then one day Wilma was in a terrible car accident that crushed her legs, her ribs, and her face. She had seventeen operations and plastic surgery. It took two years, but Wilma learned to walk again—and once she had, she went right back to work for her people. Her boss now was the Chief of the tribe, and when he took a job in Washington D.C. (as the head of the BIA), this left Wilma as the first woman Main Chief of the Cherokee Nation. Some people thought a woman shouldn't be chief, but in 1987 they held elections and Wilma Mankiller was chosen by her people to be the Chief of the Cherokee Nation. Everyone knew she could do the job.

As of 1995, Wilma is married to a full-blooded Cherokee and governs over 20,000 people. She works for good houses, good jobs, and good schools for her people. She wants the Cherokee language, arts and crafts, and culture to be strong once more.

Two hundred years ago "Mankiller" meant something like "General of the Army"; one of Wilma's ancestors liked the word so much that he took it for his name. Today, Chief Mankiller leads the Cherokee Nation in its battle against poverty, ignorance, and discrimination.

OTHER IMPORTANT PLAINS INDIANS

Red Cloud, Oglala chief and warrior

Crazy Horse, Oglala chief and warrior

Satanta (White Bear), war chief of the Kiowas, speaker

White Antelope, Cheyenne chief, warrior, peacemaker

(The four famous Native Americans mentioned above are described in *Brave Are My People, Indian Heroes Not Forgotten,* a book written by Frank Waters and published by Clear Light Publishers, Santa Fe, NM, 1993.)

White Feather, who fought at the battle of Little Big Horn

Spotted Tail, head chief of the Brule Sioux in the mid-1800's

Gall, Hunkpapa Sioux war chief, envoy to Washington D.C.

Will Rogers, Cherokee, actor, writer, and humorist

Charles Eastman, Santee Sioux, physician and writer

Maria Tallchief, Osage, ballerina

Gertrude Simmons Bonnin, Yankton Sioux, reformer and writer

Ella Carla Deloria, Yankton Sioux, linguist and scholar

N. Scott Momaday, Kiowa, author

Notes for "Historic Native Americans of the Plains and Prairies"

1. In later life Sitting Bull made a series of sixty-three autobiographical drawings. The first of these pictures of his life story shows the counting of his first coup.

2. In December 1875, The U.S. Commissioner of Indian Affairs directed all Sioux bands to come onto reservations by the end of January—or be declared hostile. Sitting Bull refused to go. Other Sioux argued that they could not meet this unrealistic deadline, as they were scattered far and wide searching for game. When General Crook attacked Chief Crazy Horse's camp, the Chief and his Oglala Sioux retreated and made their way to Sitting Bull's camp.

3. Other reports say he foretold that "soldiers would fall into his camp like grasshoppers."

4. From *Sitting Bull* by Stanley Vestal, published by Houghton Mifflin Co., 1932.

5. Jerri Terris has written a prize-winning book, *Native American Doctor: The Story of Susan LaFlesche Picotte,* which was published in 1991 by Carolrhoda Books, 241 First Avenue N., Minneapolis, MN 55401-9907.

THE PLAINS INDIANS

Activities for the Classroom

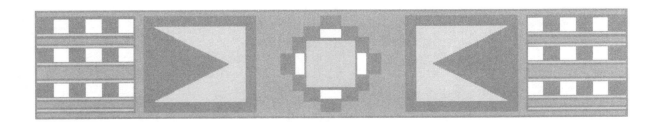

ACTIVITIES

FOOD PREPARATION

While we can neither duplicate the conditions under which Native Americans did their cooking and food preparation nor the methods (an open pit fire, a buffalo bag of hot rocks, grinding jerky in an underground mortar), we *can* encourage our students to experience and understand the processes involved in early Plains food preparation.

You can have the fun of making, and then tasting together, some of these early Native American foods.

Dried Squash

You will need: 2-3 large firm squash (butternut or summer squash); string; *optional:* chicken broth, salt, butter.

Wash, dry, and peel the squash. Slice squash horizontally in $\frac{1}{4}''$ slices, so that the middle hollow forms a hole within each slice. Remove the seeds.

String the squash slices on a piece of sturdy cord and tie this like a clothesline in a dry sunny place. Separate the squash slices so air can circulate between them.

Once dried, squash slices can be kept in a closed or covered container and then added to soups, stews, or chicken broth as it simmers. Serve warm with salt and butter.

Beef Jerky[1]

Ingredients needed: 1 $\frac{1}{2}$ lbs. brisket of beef or a large flank steak

$\frac{1}{4}$ cup soy sauce and $\frac{1}{2}$ cup water

1 tsp. garlic, freshly squeezed

$\frac{1}{2}$ cup onions, finely minced

1 Tbsp. brown sugar

(*Note*: This is a two-day process.) Partially freeze the meat to facilitate cutting. Remove all fat. Slice the meat across the grain into *thin* slices. Combine the remaining ingredients in a big bowl and place the meat strips in this liquid overnight, turning occasionally. The next day remove the meat from the liquid and shake off any excess moisture. Place these strips directly across the racks of your oven. Heat oven to 150° to 200° for 3-7 hours until the beef slices are thoroughly dried or jerked.

Beef jerky may be stored in a closed covered container (or a parfleche? . . .), but the children will probably want to begin chewing on it at once—just as Native Americans did long ago!

Four Vegetables-Mixed

This Hidatsa recipe makes about 15 small servings. You will need: 1 double handful of beans (this is a fixed quantity no matter how large a recipe you make); water; 40-50 slices of squash, dried; and 4-5 double handfuls of mixed meal (cornmeal, sunflower-seed meal), parched and pounded!

Put a (clay) pot with water "on the fire." Throw the beans into the pot. When the beans are nearly done, drop the squash slices into the cooking beans. Once the squash slices are fully cooked, remove them to a (wooden) dish and chop them with a (horn) spoon. Return the mashed squash to the beans.

Add the two meals and boil a few minutes longer (a little alkali salt might be added for seasoning, but this was unusual). The dish is ready to serve.

CRAFTS

These craft-making suggestions have been included because each provides a sense of what it was like to deal with situations met by early people. Each craft is educational *and* fun to do, and is possible to complete in a relatively short amount of time.

Sand Clay Projects

SAND CLAY RECIPE

This is a terrific recipe for clay as it produces a material that is clean to use and easy to form; it is fast drying and, once dry, rock hard! This recipe will provide a lump each for 10+ students. You will need:

2 cups sifted sand

1 cup cornstarch

1 1/2 cups cold water

Always use an old pan (from Goodwill) when preparing this recipe. Cook over medium heat, stirring constantly for 5 to 10 minutes, until mixture is very thick. (When doubled, the recipe produces a mixture that is, near completion, difficult to stir; so use a big [wooden] spoon.

Turn onto a plate and cover with a wet cloth. Cool.

Sand clay should remain moist. It may be kept for a day or two if double-bagged in plastic (tightly wrapped and tied off) and refrigerated.

Knead a bit before dividing into seperate lumps.

A Three-Dimensional Map

Prepare two double batches of Sand Clay, and cover tightly with plastic wrap.

Divide the class into pairs so that two students work together on constructing each map. Each pair of students is then given:

a large piece of foam core or heavy cardboard (scraps are often free from frame shops)

a copy of the map from the "How the First People Came Here" reproducible

white glue

toothpicks

2 plastic picnic knives

2 pencils

2 balls of Sand Clay

watercolors or poster paints

Tell the students: Study the map and, using pencils on foam core, make a *large* outline of the land masses shown on it. Next, apply some white glue to the middle area of your drawing to help anchor the clay once it is applied.

Smooth out one ball of clay onto your land mass drawing. Stay within the boundaries and smear the clay so that it is thinner near the edges of the map outline and thicker in the interior of the map.

Now, use the second ball of clay to build up the high areas, such as the Black Hills, as you refer back to the map for accurate information. Use the plastic knives and toothpicks to create crevices, rivers, plains, lakes. *Cooperate* in constructing these maps; both of you should be involved in the molding of the map contours.

Put the maps out of the way (near a heat source) and check periodically to note dryness. Once your map is dry, give it a *light* coat of watercolor; the river and lakes can be painted by using poster paints or watercolors. (Use a toothpick to apply white glue under any area that has pulled away from the cardboard.) Finally, make a neatly printed title on your map that includes the "signatures of the two cartographers."

Shelters

Sand Clay molded over margarine tubs can replicate the Earth Lodge. A twig railing around the outside of the lodge and a stick entrance hall can be added once the clay has dried.

When a variety of miniature shelters made out of paper and Sand Clay has been created, ask for volunteers to form a committee that will be responsible for organizing the student-made shelters into a classroom exhibit. Explain that you will provide any materials they request, free time in which to set up the exhibit, and that they will earn extra credit points (if these are offered in your class).

Tool Making

Provide a good supply of the following: little sticks, dead wooden matches, small scraps of wood, lots of sandpaper, scissors, white glue, markers, thin leather strips, waxed carpet thread, cotton string, small pieces of netting, needles, thread, small round rocks.

Have the students look at pictures of early Plains tools (see **Tools** section). Provide the materials listed above *and* encourage the class to bring in specific sticks or pieces of wood, shells, leather, etc., that they think would work well as (part of) a tool.

Finally, when a wide selection of materials has been collected ask each child to select a tool to faithfully and carefully replicate (in miniature, if you prefer). Give the class adequate time for this project so they will not feel rushed. Sand Clay may be used for the modeling of stone or bone elements such as bird points, scrapers, arrowheads, hoes, and ax heads.

When (a selection of) the tools has been completed, ask the class to come up with suggestions for exhibiting their work and sharing these handmade tools with other classes. Ask for a volunteer who (for extra credit) will lead the group discussion and oversee the organizing, labeling, and exhibiting of these early tool replications.

PIPESTONE PIPES

Have the children look at many pictures of different carved catlinite (pipestone) pipes.

Mix some rust-colored tempera powder—*not* liquid poster paint—into a batch of Sand Clay as it is cooking in order to achieve the color of pipestone or catlinite.

Ask the students each to draw a simple pipe, based on the pictures they have seen. The Sand Clay is used to model the short pipes, *not* the long stems that were sometimes attached to the pipe bowls.

For the lead insets in some of the Plains pipes, older students can carefully imbed very narrow strips of heavy aluminum foil at some depth below the surface of the clay.

The Sand Clay can be shaped by hand, or with an ice cream stick or a serrated plastic picnic knife. If a clay animal is attached to the short stem of the pipe, be certain the clay of the legs is made to blend *into* the clay of the pipestem, so that when the pipe dries, the animal will not fall away from the pipe itself.

Leather Projects

Look in the Yellow Pages for a leather supply store or a tannery, and inquire about obtaining quantities of (small) leather scraps. Buy a big bag for your class; it should not be expensive.

Such scraps may be used to make small versions of Plains Indian shirts, moccasins, tipis, parfleche bags, quivers, and dolls.

You can use Elmer's® Glue-all or a hot glue gun (under adult supervision) to adhere one leather surface to another, such as when making side seams on a dress or shirt. Put the glued surface under a heavy weight until the glue is dry.

Decorative designs may be added with fine-tip felt markers, stencils, and/or tempera paints.

FRINGED POUCHES

You will need two small pieces of leather about 6-inch to 7-inch square. Cut the two pieces to the same shape. Using waxed carpet thread and a heavy large-eyed needle, sew the two pieces together with a running stitch leaving a 1 $\frac{1}{2}$″ border along the two sides and the bottom (this will later become the fringe).

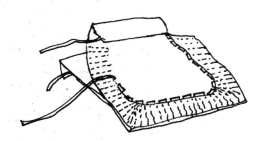

The top 1 $\frac{1}{2}$″ is folded down and hot glue is applied just along the bottom edge, leaving ample space for the leather drawstring.

Very sharp sturdy scissors are used to cut the fringe. A design may be applied to the pouch by outlining the symbol with pencil and then *carefully* coloring it in with felt markers.

THE PARFLECHE

This leather container held clothing, tools, or food such as pemmican or jerky.

You will need a piece of leather (or *heavy* brown paper) 55 inches wide and 28 inches high, narrow strips of leather for side loops, and a leather (paper) punch.

Decoration will require handmade rubber stamps and water-based linoleum block ink; or, if top flap designs are to be hand painted, tempera paints and brushes.

Cut the heavy paper or leather to this shape:

punch holes

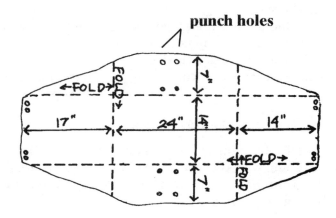

Fold along the broken lines. Punch the paper or leather at the places shown. Fold over flaps and, using leather thongs, lace flaps together.

To apply the border decoration on the front of the parfleche, open out the paper or leather so that it is flat and carefully apply the painted or rubber-stamped design as shown.

PARFLECHE BORDERS

A simple geometric pattern was often repeated on a parfleche in a border that was beaded, woven, or painted. These borders might represent clouds, bear paws, rainbows, moons. They may be hand-painted on the parfleche front flaps (using acrylic or tempera paints), or rubber stamps (as described below) can be used to create such borders.

When the paint or ink is dry, fold up the parfleche once again, fill it with pemmican or small leather articles, and then tie the side loops together.

Handmade Rubber Stamps

Contact a tire dealer that specializes in repairing truck tires. Ask the dealer to save you a damaged inner tube; there should be no charge.

Have the students study Plains Indian designs. (Dover Publications in New York offers *American Indian Design and Decoration* and *North American Indian Designs for Artists and Craftspeople*.) Choose a very simple shape that will be interesting when repeated in a line or when placed upside down in every other repetition. A 2-inch by 3-inch shape should work well.

Next, ask each child to make a pencil drawing on scrap paper of the proposed design. Once this is okayed by the teacher (as being simple and direct in design), the child transfers the design to a piece of inner tubing and next carefully cuts it out using sharp scissors. (Be sure this is done under adult supervision.)

Then the child applies airplane glue to the back side of the inner tube cutout and places this firmly onto a square of heavy corrugated cardboard that is slightly larger than the cutout itself. The glued pieces should be allowed to bond together under a heavy weight. Then the student glues a cork or an empty spool to the middle of the back of the cardboard. This will serve as a handle for the stamp.

Apply water-based printing ink to the rubber stamp with a brayer. A simpler and more direct way is to use large commercial rubber stamp pads (they are sold un-inked) that are each kept well inked with a different color (also available in office supply and craft stores). Have the child practice making rubber stamp prints on scrap paper or newsprint. Then he or she should make a row of impressions to obtain a line or border effect, on a sheet of good smooth paper, reapplying ink to the stamp when necessary.

Add to the line already designed, above and below, using the stamp straight up or inverted. Rows with alternating up and down designs can also be created. A border or all-over pattern can be made in this way. Then have the student stamp out this unique design on the cover of the parfleche bag itself.

Beading Projects

Using a beading loom is a very rewarding activity for students who already have some weaving experience and want to make such objects as beaded belts and wristguards.

MAKING AND SETTING UP THE LOOM

Use a two by four (board) of appropriate length for a base. Position finishing nails at either end to support the warp. These nails need to be very close together, so they are best staggered in two rows. The number of nails depends on how wide you want the weaving to be. If it is to be six beads wide, for example, you will need a seven-string warp (forming six rows), therefore, seven nails at each end. String the loom with a length of thin cotton string or strong thread.

Tie the string to the first nail on one end of the board and bring it down the length of the board and around behind the first and second nails at the other end. Now bring the string back up the loom to the second nail, go behind this and the third nail and back down again, around the third and fourth nail, and so on. Continue in this way until the loom is completely strung.

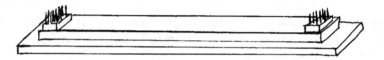

BEADING

Use rather large glass beads and long, thin beading needles. Thread the needle with a two- to three-foot strand of strong (nylon) thread. Tie the end of the thread to an outside warp string at one end of the loom. Proceed one row at a time, stringing beads on needle and thread; use as many beads at a time as there are rows between the warp strings. Pass the line of beads *under* and across the warp strings (in other words, the row of beads is perpendicular to the warp strings, not parallel with them). Using a finger, press the beads from below into position between the warp strings, then pass the (now empty) needle and thread back *through* the beads but, this time *over* the warp strings. String a second row of beads and repeat the process until you have reached the end. When it is necessary to start a new thread, tie the previous one to the warp.

If a particular pattern is desired, chart it out on graph paper using colored pencils or fine-tipped markers; each square represents a bead. Tape this paper directly below the warp strings so it may guide the beading process.

A CIGAR BOX LOOM

You can also use a cigar box as a loom. Cut slits in the sides of the box for the warp strings. The cover can be closed to protect the weaving while it is in progress, and the beads can be stored inside the box.

Paper Projects

<u>PERSONAL WINTER COUNTS</u>

To prepare for this activity give each child a large brown paper grocery bag and the following instructions: Cut the bag down the seam, across the bottom, and open it out flat. Spray or sponge on a dense covering of water over the entire bag. Wad up the sack into a tight firm ball and, finally, open it out flat to dry. (A second wetting, crushing and flattening of the paper will be helpful, though it isn't essential.) Once these papers are dry, they will have a leather-like texture. Cut each paper into a *large* animal hide. Print your name in pencil on your hide.

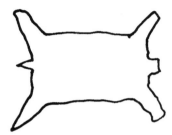

After the hides are set aside, review with your class the purpose of Winter Counts and remind them that Winter Counts are autobiographies of important leaders or warriors, or the historic records of a tribe. Show the class the two formats for these Counts: (1) circular, beginning at center of hide and reading in a spiral outward, and (2) linear, reading left to right and top to bottom.

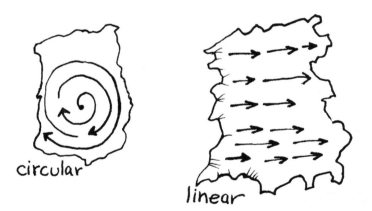

Point out how the glyphs or pictographs stand for words and ideas. Then encourage the students to come up with a short list of ten to twelve important (happy) times in their lives. These could be things they have enjoyed doing, playing with, eating, or places they have gone, or things they have had fun seeing or hearing. Once this list is made, have each child create a glyph (small pictograph) to stand for each of the 10 to 12 events. Encourage the children to occasionally repeat some of the glyphs, or use them in a new way, e.g., a head that stands for the student may occur often, or a series of crescent moons may be used to mean time passed.

Once the children have designed their Winter Counts, they get back the brown paper hides they prepared earlier. Each then uses a pencil to transfer the personal Winter Count to the hide using either a spiral or linear format. Next the glyphs are darkened with fine-point felt markers or with watercolors.

Display the Winter Counts in the room and occasionally ask for someone to volunteer to come up to the display and describe his or her pictographs and the events they illustrate.

Ghost Dance Shirt

(To understand the meaning of this shirt, see note 6 in **The Europeans Come**.)

You will need: white paper, large sheets of (heavy) brown wrapping or mural paper, pencils, scissors, glue, tempera paints and brushes, (marking pens). You may provide several large tagboard patterns of the shirt shape shown if you want consistency of shape (or the students may each draw their shirt shape on the paper from a life-size shirt outline you make on the chalkboard).

Once the student has a shirt drawn on the paper, he or she paints in a personal design, cuts out the shirt, and glues on lots of long thin fringe and carefully made "eagle feathers."

These shirts will make an outstanding classroom display.

INDIVIDUAL HAND-SIZED STUDENT TIMELINES

Here is an excellent way to reinforce historical information which you want your class to remember. This technique also aids sequential thinking and is a very good mnemonic device.

You will need: 5″ × 8″ file cards (three for each student plus extra for errors), paper cutter, rulers, pencils, a rubber band for each student, 1-inch wide cellophane tape, markers/crayons, glue, scissors, wildlife magazines, and several table knives.

Preparing the Blank Timelines

Mark each file card lengthwise at $2\,{}^5\!/_8''$ intervals at top and bottom.

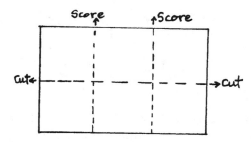

Now use a ruler and the back of the blade of a table knife to connect the first two marks top and bottom; this will score the file card so that it may later be neatly folded. Connect the second set of two marks with a score line also. (This will create two vertical lines and three columns on the card.)

Then, carefully cut each card in half lengthwise. (Each card will now be two 2 $\frac{1}{2}$″ × 8″ strips, with three sections in each strip, for a total of six sections.)

Using the Blank Timelines

Demonstrate how to neatly tape two strips (six sections) of a timeline together.

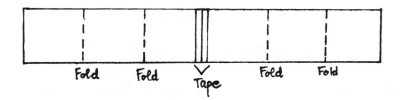

Each student tapes the two strips together to form the beginning of the individual timeline; then he or she designs an appropriate title section (cover) for the timeline using the words and dates: *Native Americans of the Plains and Prairies (23,000 B.C. to A.D. 1800)*. Each prints his or her name neatly in tiny letters somewhere on this first section, and then folds the timeline accordion-like, with the cover showing on top, and secures it closed with a rubber band.

Collect these blank timelines and return them to the students once you have studied: *23,000-11,000 B.C. Siberians Cross Bering Strait into North America*. Each will make a drawing* (on the empty section next to their title section) to illustrate the Siberians coming over to North America and note the date. Collect the timelines and then return them to the students after you have studied: *7,500-4,500 B.C. Prehistoric Bison Hunters on the Plains and Prairies*. Children each make a picture with magazine cutouts and/or drawings to illustrate the big game hunters in North America. Continue this procedure after the introduction of (each of) the important historical date(s). When five dates have been illustrated, you will need to provide each student with a new index card. Repeat the procedure described above (scoring, cutting, taping) and connect this new part of the timeline to the first part. (Since there are more than eleven sections required to complete this particular timeline, you will have to go through this procedure once more, later, in order to finish this project.)

*Some students may also want to show the Native Americans being put on Earth by Old Men, or coming up out of a sacred lake, or down from the sky: Creation-in-place theory.

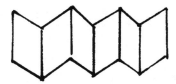

Before adding (a) new date(s) to the timelines, have the class quickly read through the dates that have already been noted. Repeating the dates, starting with 23,000 B.C., each time a new date is added will offer good oral review and will help cement the sequential dates in their minds.

Collect the timelines after new addition(s) are made and store them in a specific place. This protects the timelines and keeps the images fresh for the students.

When the timelines covering 23,000 B.C. to A.D. 1800 are completed, neatly display them (in the hallway) at the children's eye-level, using straight pins or double-stick tape on the *back* (not staples, or tape on the front, which would damage the timelines). This will encourage the students to review the dates.

Depending on the time you have, and the emphasis you want to give the 18th to 20th centuries, you may choose to have the children make a large classroom timeline: *Native Americans of the Plains and Prairies* A.D. *1725 to . . .*

Dates

The following dates can be used to make a timeline for the Native Americans of the Plains and Prairies:

Creation-in-place (coming (up) out of a natural site): the Native American view of the arrival of the first people to this continent.

c. 23,000 B.C. to c. 11,000 B.C.	The first people come to North America; they use the Bering Strait to cross over to this continent
c. 7500-4500 B.C.	Prehistoric bison hunters on the Plains; they dry meat, mix it with berries, and store it in hide or gut containers
c. 500 A.D.	Bow and arrow
1000-1250 A.D.	Farming villages of the Prairies, middle Plains; along Missouri to North Dakota
c. 1250 A.D.	Drought drives out the farmers
c. 1350 A.D.	People begin to drift back to the Prairies; most become farmers who do some hunting
1500s	Shoshoni come into Wyoming; Apache come into Colorado; Blackfeet come into northwest Plains; walled villages are built along the rivers
1540	Coronado and his men come to Wichita towns (in present-day Kansas)
1700-75	Plains Indians begin to use and trade *horses*

c. 1700-1800	*The Golden Age of the Plains Indians*
1725	Sioux and Cheyenne come into North Dakota
1780-1900s	Epidemics (smallpox, measles, cholera) among tribes
1780-1800	Smallpox and cholera among Texas tribes
1800	Cheyenne are nomadic hunters on the plains
1824	Bureau of Indian Affairs (BIA) is organized as part of the U.S. Department of War
1825	Indian Country (lands west of the Mississippi River) is created
1829-90	Fighting between U.S. Army and Plains Indians
1830	Indian Removal Act (IRA) is passed to relocate eastern Indians (including Cherokee) to west of the Mississippi River
1832	Supreme Court rules IRA wrong but President Andrew Jackson ignores ruling
1837-70	Smallpox epidemics hit Mandan, Hidatsa, and Arikara
1838-39	Cherokee Trail of Tears
1848-49	California Gold Rush
1850-60	Cholera epidemic among tribes in southern plains
1853-54	The northern part of Indian Territory becomes the states of Kansas and Nebraska
1853-56	U.S. Government gets 174,000,000 acres of Indian land through 52 treaties, all eventually broken by U.S.
1861-65	*U.S. Civil War*
1866	Railroad Act takes American Indian lands for railroad use. Homestead Act opens up Kansas and Nebraska lands for homesteading
1867-83	Whites kill thirteen million buffalo
1869	Transcontinental railroad is completed
1876, June 26	Battle at Little Big Horn, where Cheyenne, Sioux, and Arapaho defeat U.S. forces (*Custer's Last Stand*)
1885	Last great herd of buffalo is destroyed; Peyote religion begins among Kiowa and Comanche
1885-90	Smallpox epidemic on the reservations
1887	Dawes Act: reservation lands are divided; over a hundred reservations are created. American Indians lose millions of acres of land; they have gone from living in all of North America to living on 4% of the United States

1889	Ghost Dance religion spreads in the Plains
1890, December 15	Sitting Bull is killed following a dispute with federal troops
1890, December 29	The last battle in the U.S.-Indian wars, *The Wounded Knee Massacre*, takes place in South Dakota. 350 Sioux on way to Ghost Dance are killed by U.S. troops
1898	Curtis Act does away with tribal governments
1909	President Theodore Roosevelt makes two and a half million acres of wooded Indian reservation lands into national forests
1915	Native American (Peyote) Church incorporated
1917-19	*World War I*: Native Americans enlist into armed services
1924	Indian Citizenship Act: all Native Americans born in the U.S. become American citizens
1930s	The Depression; Dust Bowl droughts
1934	Indian Reorganization Act
1941-45	*World War II*: Native Americans enter U.S. services, industry
1950s	Relocation of Native Americans from reservations to cities
1968	Indian Civil Rights Act: gives Native Americans right to self-government on reservations
1973	Members of American Indian Movement (AIM) take over trading post at Wounded Knee, South Dakota (site of 1890 massacre) to draw attention to the situation of American Indians today
1988	Indian Gaming Regulatory Act
1989	University of Nebraska agrees to return to the Omaha tribe more than one hundred tribal skeleton remains the University had had for a hundred years
1990	Native American Grave Protection and Reparation Act: protects American Indian grave sites and requires the return to tribes of identifiable remains and sacred burial objects

ZIP AROUND (A CLASSROOM GAME)

This is a game that can quickly teach children, in grades 4–6, important background facts about the Plains Indians.

The format of this game, developed by Julie Wheeler of Portland, Oregon, can be used to learn and review facts in any subject area—and the students love it! The fact that they compete as a group against their *own* best record as a group also makes it exciting.

The goal of the game is to help students *quickly* gain a body of background information on the Plains Indians.

To play "Zip Around," each student is given a card; immediately assure them that this is not a test and that it doesn't require them to answer the question on their card! Ask them if there are any numbers or words on their card that they cannot pronounce. Give them any needed pronunciations.

One student begins by asking the question on the bottom of his or her card. (The first time the game is played, no one will try to go fast. Use this as a dry run to familiarize students with the game's structure. Successive games will be timed.) The student whose card has the answer to this first question reads it out (no raised hands are needed to signal the response) and then reads the question at the bottom of his or her card. In this way, all the questions are asked and answered, eventually coming back to the player who started the game.

Collect and shuffle the cards so that now, for the second round, students will receive different cards and learn different facts. Time the students; later they can see if they can beat this time. Shuffle the cards and try again. (Two students may read from one card if you like, and you may pair a strong reader with a weak reader to offer peer assistance.) Stop play after 2–4 rounds. Play again in a day or so.

"Zip Around" cards are 7″ × 8″ pieces of posterboard with the following printed strips glued on them, one statement and one question on each of 22 cards.

Susan LaFlesche was the first Native American to become a medical doctor.

What crops did the farming tribes raise?

The farming tribes raised corn, bean, and squash.

What animals did the nomadic tribes hunt?

The nomadic tribes hunted buffalo, deer and antelope.

What wild plants did the Plains people use for food?

The Plains people ate wild berries, turnips, and milkweed.

What material did they use for their clothes?

They made their clothing from deer and buffalo skins.

What kind of houses did the Plains people live in?

The nomadic tribes lived in tipis and the farming tribes lived in earth lodges and grass-covered huts.

Who was Quanah Parker?

Quanah Parker was the last great Plains prophet. He helped start the Native American Church.

What is the Sun Dance?

The Sun Dance is a ceremony held in summer to honor nature and the Great Spirit.

What is a medicine bundle?

A medicine bundle is a personal collection of objects thought to have healing powers.

Before the Europeans came to North America, where did most of the Plains tribes live?

In early times most of the Plains tribes lived along rivers and streams because the soil there was good for farming.

Why did the Plains people use sign language?

Sign language was helpful when trading with people who did not speak your language.

What are the names of some Plains Indian tribes?

Some names of Plains Indian tribes are the Sioux, the Comanche, the Crow, the Blackfeet.

What are the names of some Plains Indian languages?

Some names of Plains Indian languages are: Siouan, Caddoan, and Algonquin.

What did the farming tribes trade with the nomadic tribes?

The farming tribes traded dried squash, corn, and berries to the nomadic tribes.

How did the horse change the lives of the Plains Indians?

The horse could carry heavy loads and travel very far, so it let Plains people ride after buffalo and on raids to other villages.

What was a parfleche?

A parfleche was a leather container that held dried food or other small objects.

What was a travois?

A travois was made of two long poles tied to the sides of a dog or horse. Big bundles tied to these poles were dragged along by the animal.

What is quillwork?

Porcupine quills are dyed, flattened, and woven into (quillwork) designs.

What was a Winter Count?

> *A Winter Count was a picture calendar of an important leader's life, or the record of a tribe.*
>
> *Where do most Native Americans live today?*

> *Today more than half of all Native Americans live in cities.*
>
> *What did the buffalo give to the Native Americans?*

> *Food, clothing, houses, and tools all came to the Plains Indian from the buffalo.*

> *Sitting Bull was a famous Sioux medicine man who helped to lead the Plains Indians to victory at Custer's Last Stand.*
>
> *Who was Susan LaFlesche?*

EARLY PLAINS INDIAN GAMES[2]

Here is a collection of games played by the Plains people that you may enjoy playing with your students.

The Blindfold Game

This game was used long ago to test a brave's ability to sense direction correctly.

Stand with the group on a flat open area. Have one student, the target, stand 25 feet away from the group. Then blindfold another child, and gently spin this student around a few times and aim him or her toward the student who is standing away from the group. The blindfolded student must try to reach the target player who does not move from his or her spot (but who may occasionally make a soft sound).

Once everyone (including you) has had a turn, ask the players to share their success secrets with the group ("I listened for sounds to tell me where I was going," or "I tried to feel the warmth of the sun," and so on). Talk together about how such variables would relate to a Native American tracking an animal in the wild or finding the way home in the dark.

Animal Imitations

During their ceremonial dances, and before going on a buffalo hunt, Plains people imitated bison and other wild creatures.

Pairs of children may imitate the same animal or one may pretend to be some other element in nature. Emphasize that they should try and show many details about their chosen creature and its life; they should not just do one action over and over again.

Explain that all guesses are to be withheld until the entire imitation is completed. Only then, by raising their hands, can the students try to identify the creature that has just been imitated.

Hop Race

Draw a line on the ground; draw a second line 30 or 40 feet away. (Two) players stand behind the first line and at the sound of a bell or a drum, the (two) players hop on their right feet all the way to the distant line, where they turn around and hop on their left feet all the way back to the starting line; now they turn around and hop on both feet back to the distant line. The first player over that line counts coup and receives a large paper eagle feather.

Later the children might enjoy playing a more challenging version of this game in which all the actions are repeated as above, plus the added detail that the hopping players must hold their other foot with their hand as they are hop-racing! This requires additional balance and coordination.

Jump Race

Draw a line on the ground; draw another line 60 feet away. The (2-15) players line up four feet apart just behind the line. Holding their feet tight together they follow this pattern: jump to the left, then jump to the right, and then jump as far forward as possible. Next jump to the right, then jump to the left, and finally jump as far forward as possible. This pattern must be repeated over and over until each player gets to the finish line.

If a player jumps in a wrong pattern, he or she must turn around and take three big jumps back toward the starting line before continuing to jump toward the finish line.

The first player to reach the finish line, having always jumped in the correct pattern, or having taken any necessary backwards jumps, counts coup and receives a paper eagle feather.

This race can also be played as a relay race with three players jumping in pattern to the distant line where another teammate is tagged and so on. The winning team members all count coup!

Whirl and Catch

This game is best played outside during recess. Each player has four to ten thin 4-inch long sticks (bamboo skewers sold at grocery stores can be cut to 4-inch lengths). At first, players will only use three or four of these sticks. As their skill improves, they will begin adding more sticks to their play until at last they may be able to handle all ten sticks!

Place three sticks on the back of your hand, which is held at about waist level. Toss the sticks straight up in the air a bit above your head. Catch the falling sticks on the palm of that same hand. You must keep your fingers outstretched as you catch the sticks or the catch doesn't count. If you are successful using three sticks, go on to using four, and so on, until you miss. At this point the second player has a turn.

Variations include: catch the falling sticks with the same back of the hand that tossed them up; toss the sticks up into the air, whirl around, and catch the falling sticks on the back of your hand.

The Stone Game

This game develops memory and observation skills and may improve the children's SAT scores!

For each pair of players you will need: 30 small stones, some light and some dark in color, and in a variety of shapes; a watch with a second hand; a set of large file cards or pieces of tagboard on which the following patterns are shown with one pattern in large images on each card:

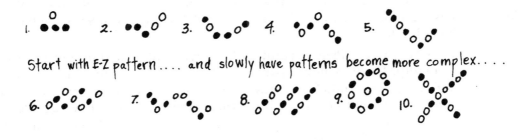

This game may be played by one, two, or more players. If two are playing, the second child turns over one of the cards, revealing a pattern, and then times the first player who studies the card for just one (or two) minutes, at which point the second player removes the card from sight. Then the first player, using the stones, tries to reproduce the pattern shown on the card. This pattern is checked against the pattern on the card. If the patterns match, the first player is congratulated and takes over the job of the second player; if the patterns do not match, the first player arranges the stones to duplicate the card's pattern and THEN takes on the new role, while the former second player now studies the new card pattern. The game continues as long as the two players are interested in playing.

CREATIVE WRITING (OR JOURNAL-ENTRY) SUGGESTIONS

The following may be used as themes for oral readings, creative writing self-starters, or jointly written pieces:

1. Imagine yourself as one of the first Asians who crossed the Bering Straits into North America. Name several things you saw on your walk. What kinds of thoughts did you have? What were you looking forward to? Why would it be a better life for you in this new land?

2. At the top of your paper, write *Sitting in My Tipi* (or *In My Earth House* or *In My Grass House*). Imagine that you are a Plains Indian. Think about exactly what is in your home; you may want to make a list of the things. Then write a description of the inside of your home and include each thing on your list. Add lots of details such as colors, the number of things, any paintings there may be, who sleeps and works in each part of the shelter, and so on. Make the inside of your home come alive to the reader.

3. A eulogy is a poem that praises its subject (its beauty, nobility, strength, and so on); this kind of poem does not need to rhyme. Write a eulogy for the American Buffalo. Praise many different things about this animal and say why it deserves to have a eulogy written for it.

4. Coyote is a creator *and* a trickster; he is wise *and* cunning. He makes things happen— sometimes he is too smart for his own good so he ends up being ridiculous. Make up a Coyote tale to explain how Coyote got his pointed nose, for example, or how he brought the buffalo to the Great Plains . . . or . . . ? Your choice! Have fun!

5. Imagine yourself to be a young Plains Indian child. Think about "your favorite toy," e.g., a top, throwing sticks, a doll, bow and arrows, bullroarer, clay dishes (or later, a play horse). Make up a short story that includes: a detailed description of your toy; who made it; why you first wanted it; why, in particular, you love it; and how you first learned to use it. Finally, tell what became (or will become) of this special part of your Plains Indian childhood.

6. Study a map of the Great Plains. Think of how you could use different places on the map to tell a story. Maybe you are part of a war party going out to meet the enemy. Perhaps you are a child riding in a travois going to a new camp, or you might be a member of a party going to trade with another tribe. Once you have decided on the person you are, make up a story that uses some of the names of places on your map. Include a hand-drawn map that shows everywhere "you" went in your story.

7. Plains women and men sometimes got their names from something that happened to them (Crooked Foot, Runs Away with his Horses, or Left Hand Tied Behind Him). Sometimes they got their names from something they did (Red-colored Corn Woman or Falling Down Woman). Think about yourself: what is something you have done—or something that has happened to you—that is important enough to suggest a name for yourself? Write this name at the top of your paper; then explain how this name came to be "given" to you.

8. Brainstorm with your class or with a friend to create a list of experiences that an Indian pony might have. These might include various ways in which a horse might reach the Plains; who its owners were; how it was treated and used; (mis)adventures that it had; what its daily life was like. Use this list to help get a (group) story started. Write your story in the first person and try to make it as original (filled with the unexpected) as you can!

9. "Going on a Name Quest," a creative thinking and writing activity: You will need 25 to 35 large file cards; on each card glue a small colorful, engaging picture of an animal, snake, bird, or sea creature. Explain to the class that a Name Quest was taken by young Plains children in order to find a new name or a personal animal helper.

   Place the picture cards face down and have each child pick a card at random. Then each student quietly studies the picture he or she drew. There must be absolute silence so that each person's mind may be able to take the child on a quest for a new name! Encourage the children to come up with details about their creature and the time they spent together.

   These adventures can be shared orally or put into writing and into personal drawings. Encourage the students to really "see, hear, touch, and smell the place they go to" and tell them to "have courage" to go through their quest and return with a new name!

CULMINATING ACTIVITY: CREATING A MUSEUM OF THE PLAINS AND PRAIRIES

When your third- to eighth-grade students have completed their studies of Native Americans, discuss with them how your class might share with others the things you've been doing in the past weeks.

If the idea of constructing a classroom museum appeals to the group, start off by making a class-generated list defining what a museum *is,* and the many kinds of things you can find there. Next have them list all the things they have made during their studies (tools, food, beading, various crafts, Winter Counts, timelines, and so on). Help them decide how they might best exhibit these.

Next, help them brainstorm how their museum could appeal to all the senses! This could include: *Taste*—dried fruit and vegetables, pemmican; *Smell*—sweetgrass, leather, smoke; *Touch*—Plains' objects, each inside a sock in a shoe box with the lid taped shut; an identifying label could be in the form of a riddle.

Hand goes in here

Hear—tape, sound effects, Native American instruments; *Sight*—video, slides, signs, folktale collections; and *Make*—replicas, Sand Clay objects, and so on.

Finally, organize committees to each take responsibility for a specific aspect of your museum. This might involve categories such as: large signs, labels for exhibits, displays of specific objects (shelters or crafts), the large timeline, and so on; let them come up with the specific categories. Then ask for volunteers for each category (committee) and let these children organize themselves, targeting tasks to be done and how best to accomplish them. Each committee should make a list of materials they will need to complete their work. See that these materials are provided.

If at all possible, the students should visit a local museum and keep a list of all the physical elements "a good museum" should have, e.g., well-written labels and signs, intriguing objects, a clear chronology, thought-provoking exhibits, a few unexpected (manipulatives or action-oriented) displays, and so on.

When their museum is completed, invite the public, and open the doors!

OTHER SUGGESTIONS FOR CULMINATING ACTIVITIES

1. A time capsule is a container made to hold and preserve major elements of a historic period or culture. It is filled, and then buried or put into a vault until a much later time (centuries later, perhaps) when it is opened and its contents are studied. Time capsules originated in the 20th century, but if you had lived in 1775 on the Great Plains, and you had a vision that told you to collect things to be placed in a jar for future children to see, what things would you have chosen? Make a list of things that represent the Plains Indian culture. Be sure to include examples of food, clothing, tools, children, arts and crafts, religion, war, and so on.

   Make an X-ray picture of the filled jar—as if you were able to see through the sides of the jar and could see all the things in it. Show all the details!

2. At the end of their Native American studies, have each student list: *Five Things I Didn't Know Before We Studied the Plains Tribes.* (You could have them make a second list, if you like: *Some Things I Still Don't Know about the Plains Indians . . . and Wish I DID . . .*)

   As the unit is in progress, you might want to tell your class: "At the end of our Native American studies, I will want each of you to tell me one thing you still don't know concerning the Plains people, but would like to (have) learn(ed)." This exercise will help you see where their areas of interest lie —and may help you in planning a "Native Americans of the Plains and Prairies" unit for next year!

Notes for "Activities for the Classroom"

1. To jerk means to preserve by drying. We got our word "jerky" from the Spanish *charki* (char-kee), a word the conquistadores encountered in Perú, where it means "meat dried in strips."

2. Many of these games are described in *Handbook of American Indian Games* by Allen and Paulette McFarlan, published by Dover Publications, Inc., NY, 1958.

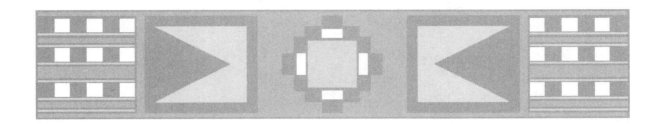

THE PLAINS INDIANS

Ready-to-Use
Reproducible Activities

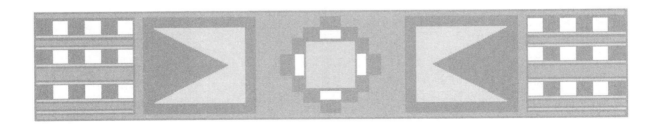

Name _____

HOW THE FIRST PEOPLE CAME HERE

This is a picture of the land we live in: North America.

Long, long ago no people lived here. Ice covered much of the land. The ice made a bridge so people could cross over to the land we live in today.

Many scientists believe that the first people came here from Siberia.

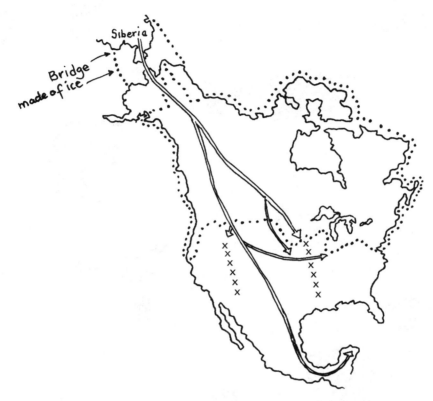

1. Use a white crayon to cover all the places the ice covered. This is marked by . • . •   • . • • .

2. (Ask your teacher to help you) find where you live in North America. Mark it with a ☆

3. Use green to outline the Great Plains and Prairies. They are marked by x x× × × x × ×ˣ

4. Make a long orange arrow to show where scientists think people came from Siberia, through Canada, down to the Great Plains.

Many Native Americans do not believe this. Their old songs and stories say that the first people were put on the plains by Old Man (Crow), or that they came from the sky (Osage). This is what they believe.

Name _____

CAN YOU FIND THE TWINS?

Draw a line between each pair of twins. Then you can color all the twins.

A PICTURE COUNT

Count the things you see and put the number in the circle.

A MEDICINE SHIELD

A medicine shield had a picture on it to bring a man good luck. Make a picture on this shield. Use an animal *you* like a lot. Draw some little signs around the edge of your shield. Draw eagle feathers hanging down from 1 side *or* make a long red ribbon going around it!

THE TIPI

Cut out each tipi. Glue the 1 side under the opposite side to form a
You can glue toothpicks inside the top for lodge poles.

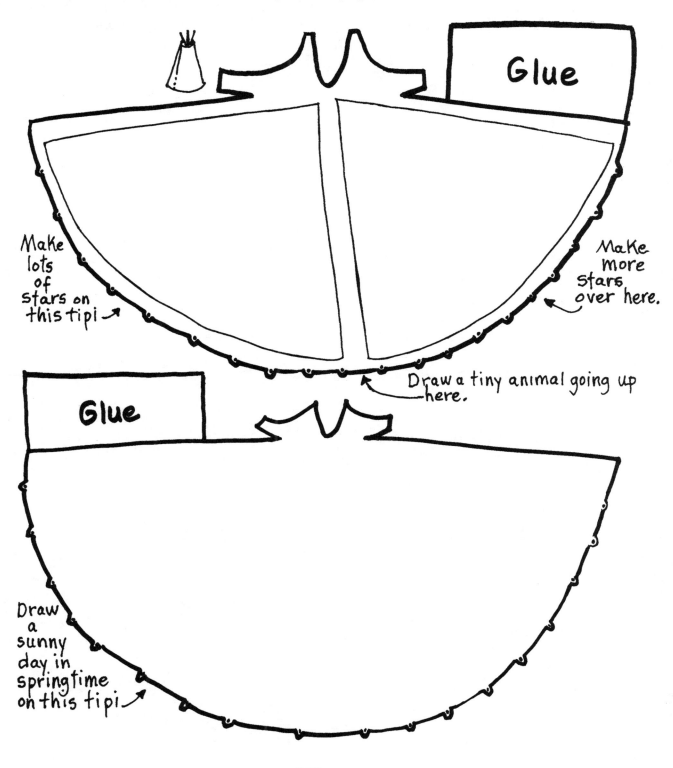

Glue

Make lots of stars on this tipi →

Make more stars over here. ←

Draw a tiny animal going up here. ←

Glue

Draw a sunny day in springtime on this tipi →

A GRASS HOUSE

The early Plains people in the south made their houses out of woven grass and sticks. Draw a Grass House in the ⠒⠒⠒ below. Make three trees by it. Draw a garden in front of it. Show a river nearby. Then draw some of the animals that lived in the south: rabbits, fox, birds, deer, fish, bear, squirrels, and snakes. Color your picture.

MAKE A PARFLECHE

This leather bag was called a parfleche. It was used by the Plains Indians to hold food or clothes.

Using a pencil, start at 1. Then go to 2 and then to 3. Keep going until you get to 12!

Then make one of these designs

all over your bag. Color your bag and use ONLY red, green, and/or yellow.

1.
9•
•2
•3

8• •12
7•
•5
6•

100-YEAR-OLD PLAINS INDIAN VEST

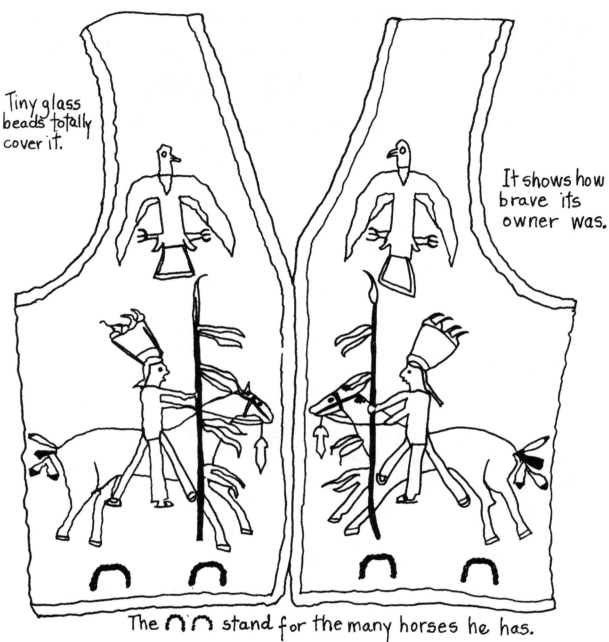

Tiny glass beads totally cover it.

It shows how brave its owner was.

© 1995 by The Center for Applied Research in Education

The ⋒⋒ stand for the many horses he has.

Color the eagles: golden brown and white.
Color the horses: grey.
Color the edges of the vest: red.
Leave the background of the vest white. Make the rest of the vest colorful.
Now write a story about how the owner got this wonderful vest!

Name _____

A GRASS HOUSE MAZE

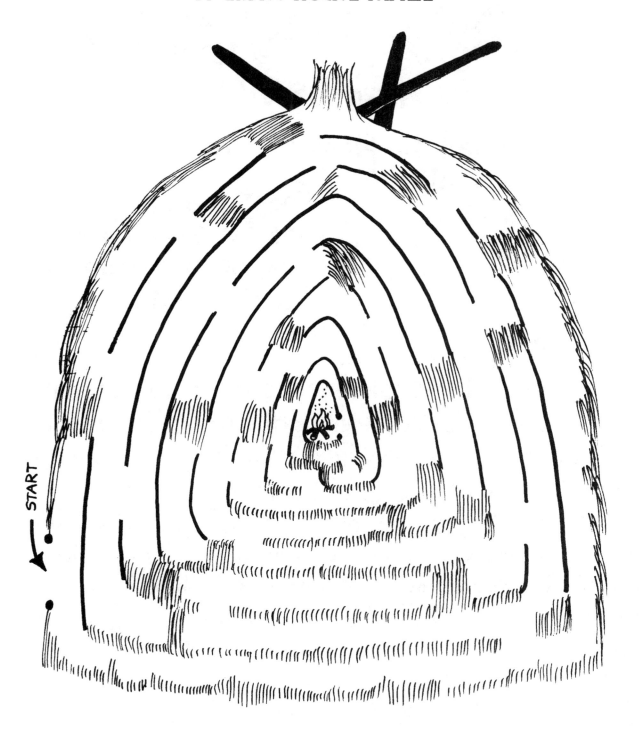

START

A maze is a long hidden path. This grass house of the southern Plains has a maze inside it. Use a pencil to show how to get from the door to the fire in the middle of the house. Good luck!

Sunflower Seed Balls

shelled sunflower seeds
(corn oil)
(salt)

toaster-oven
mortar(s) & pestle(s)
  OR electric food grinder
cookie sheets

© 1995 by The Center for Applied Research in Education

Wash your hands.

Toast the shelled seeds in the toaster oven.

Use a pestle to grind the seeds in a mortar (or you can use an electric food grinder). Make the seeds into a powder. (Add salt to your taste.)

Add <u>drops</u> of oil to this powder just until the meal sticks together and makes a dough. Take about a Tablespoon of the dough and with your hands press it into a round firm ball. Put this ball on a cookie sheet.

These Sunflower Seed Balls gave quick energy to Plains Indians on long trips......YOU can enjoy one at snack time!

Name _____

GETTING TO KNOW THE GREAT PLAINS

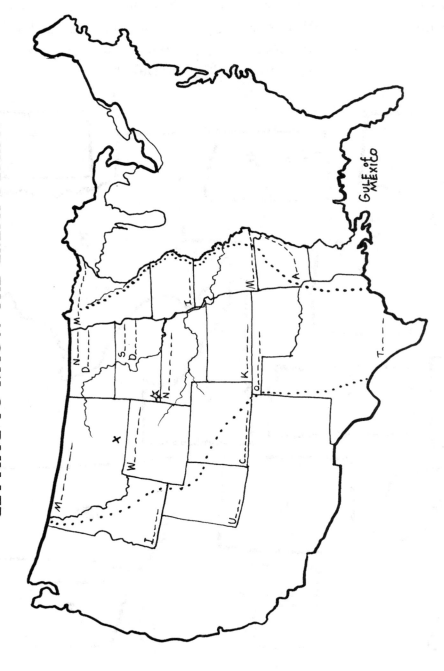

Use small letters to fill in the names of each Plains state. The little dots show the two sides of the Great Plains. The eastern side is the Mississippi River. It begins in Minnesota and runs into the Gulf of Mexico. Mark it in GREEN. The western side of the Plains is along the Rocky Mountains. Make small XXX all along the western side of the plains and mark these: ROCKY MTS.

The Missouri River comes off the Mississippi River and runs up into Montana. Mark it in blue and label it MISSOURI RIVER. The Platte River comes off the Missouri River and runs into Nebraska. Label it PLATTE RIVER. See the ☆ on the map. Label this BLACK HILLS. Label the X LITTLE BIG HORN. Now you know more about the Great Plains!

Name _____

THE PLAINS STATES

Look at the shapes below. Can you tell which Plains state each shape is? Put the correct number in front of the name of each state.

____ Arkansas   ____ Kansas   ____ Nebraska   ____ Texas
____ Colorado   ____ Minnesota   ____ N. Dakota   ____ Utah
____ Idaho   ____ Missouri   ____ Oklahoma   ____ Wyoming
____ Iowa   ____ Montana   ____ S. Dakota

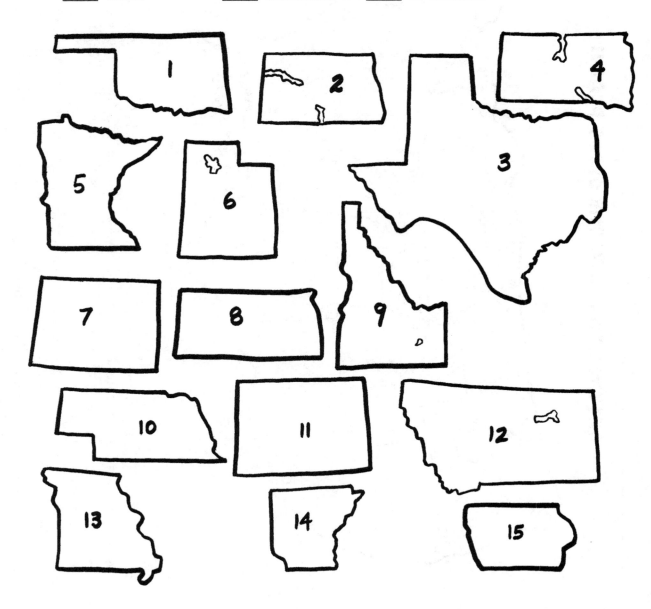

(You may want to look back at your *Getting to Know the Great Plains* worksheet!)

THE GRASS HOUSE

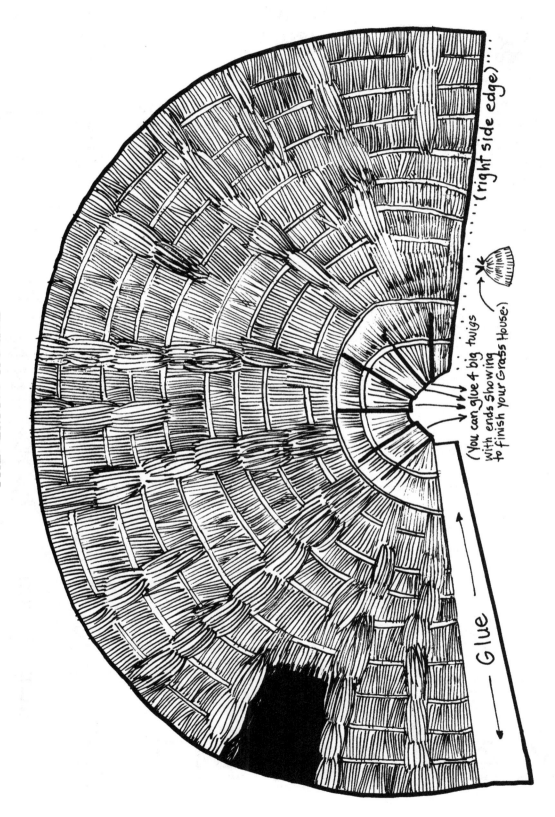

(right side edge).......

(You can glue 4 big twigs
with ends showing
to finish your Grass House.)

Glue

Use watercolors or crayons to color the horizontal sticks dark brown and the vertical grasses light green. Cut along the heavy lines. Put glue on the place that says **Glue.** Swing the glued edge under the right-side edge and glue in place. Glue four twigs sticking out of the top hole as shown above to complete your grass house!

ARAPAHO SYMBOLS

SWALLOW

BUFFALO SKULL

PERSON

PERSON

LIFE

SUN

LIZARD

BEAR-FOOT

MORNING STAR

CONSTELLATION

The Arapaho used these symbols instead of the written word. Make up an adventure story that uses as many of these symbols as you can. Use written words to complete each sentence. (You may have to continue your tale on another piece of paper.) Have FUN!

CATERPILLAR

CLOUD

LIGHTNING

BUTTERFLY

ROCKS

CRICKET

MOUNTAINS

TURTLE

RIVER

SPIDER

RIVER WITH ISLANDS

THUNDER-BIRD

PATH

ARROW-POINT

PARFLECHE

TIPI

CENTER

INTERIOR OF TIPI

CAMP CIRCLE

CROSSING PATHS

PATH GOING OVER A HILL

© 1995 by The Center for Applied Research in Education

172

EARLY PLAINS INDIAN DOLL AND CLOTHING

Carefully color and cut these out. Have fun playing with your paper doll!

Sioux doll

Blackfeet c.1875

cut out

Shoshone c.1890

Sioux 19th cent.

EARLY PLAINS INDIAN DOLL AND CLOTHING

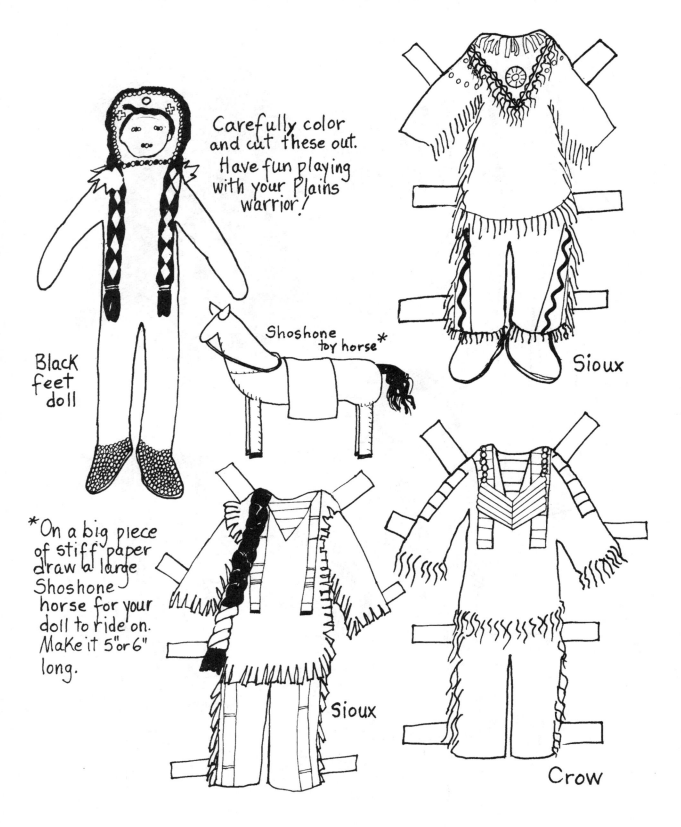

Carefully color and cut these out. Have fun playing with your Plains warrior!

Black feet doll

Shoshone toy horse*

Sioux

*On a big piece of stiff paper draw a large Shoshone horse for your doll to ride on. Make it 5" or 6" long.

Sioux

Crow

174

Name _____

ABC FOLLOW-THE-DOTS

Using a pencil, start at A and go to B. Keep on going until you get to Z.

This is an early Sioux Indian drawing of a buffalo.
Color it brown.
Make thick grass for it to eat.
Then show what kind of day it is.

175

YOUR VISION QUEST

You have been out on this high hill for 4 days and nights without food—or water—or sleep. Then you have a great dream! Draw here what you see. Be sure to show what animal comes to you. Show LOTS of DETAILS.

(Museum of New Mexico, Negative 16101)

When you finish with your drawing, write about "your experience" and explain how you felt about it.

Name _____

Here is what the BUFFALO .... gave us!

Hair _____

Horns _____

Skull _____

Tongue _____

Bones _____

Stomach Lining _____

Intestines _____

Flesh _____

Neck pelt _____

Bladder _____

Heart _____

Hide _____

Tail _____

Ribs _____

Fat _____

Tendons _____

Hooves _____

Sinew _____

Marrow _____

Fill in as MANY of the blanks as you *can*.
Here are a few hints: bucket • sled • glue • spoon • dice • knife • rattle • soap • stuffing • shield • rope • fly switch.

Pemmican

lean beef jerky: 20+ strips
melted butter (corn oil)
dried tart cherries (sold at health food
(or dried cranberries)   grocery stores)

mortars & pestles
(or a blender)
serrated plastic knives
big bowl(s)

Wash your hands.
Take off any fat from the beef jerky.
Use the mortar(s) and pestle(s) (or the blender) to grind up the jerky into a powder.
Add just enough butter or oil to make the powder into a smooth paste.
Use the plastic knives to chop up the berries: not too fine.
Add the berries to the meat paste.
Mix well. Store in a parfleche... or other cool dry place!

The Plains Indians ate pemmican throughout the winter months when fresh meat was scarce.

© 1995 by The Center for Applied Research in Education

Name _____

WHERE THE TRIBES WERE LIVING IN ABOUT 1600!

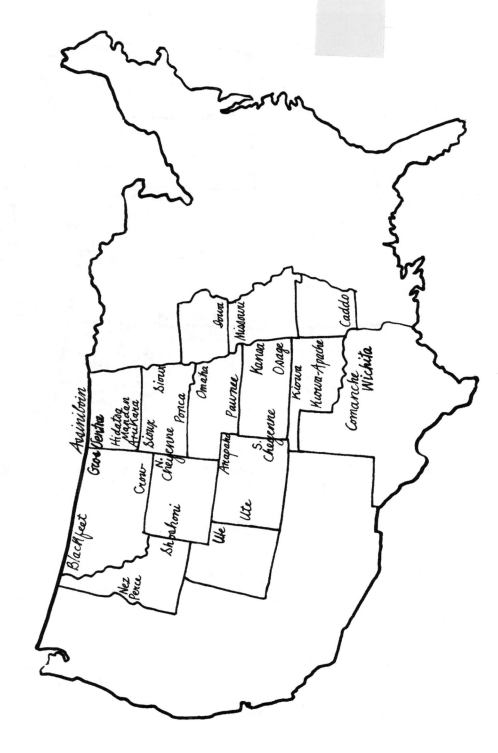

Look at this map.

Then compare it with "The Reservations" map worksheet.

Find the ten tribes that no longer live in the area where they first lived. List them on the back of this sheet. Then write where they lived in about 1600 and where their reservation(s) is (are) today.

THE RESERVATIONS

Look at this map of the Plains states. Write the name(s) of the state(s)* in the blank(s) to show where that tribe's reservations are found TODAY.

TRIBES:

Apache _____   Gros Ventre _____   Pawnee _____

Arapaho _____   Hidatsa _____   Ponca _____

Arikara _____   Iowa _____   Shoshoni _____

Assiniboin _____ Kiowa _____   Sioux _____

Blackfeet _____   Mandan _____   _____

Caddo _____   Missouri _____   _____

Cheyenne _____   Nez Perce _____   Ute _____

Comanche _____   Omaha _____   Wichita _____

Crow _____   Osage _____

                       Oto _____

*You can use abbreviations if you want: CO, ID, IA, KS, MN, MO, MT, NE, ND, OK, SD, WY.

LEDGER DRAWING PUZZLE

CAREFULLY cut out each picture square. Glue it in the blank square that has the same number. When you have done this with all the squares, you will have a Plains Indian Ledger Drawing!

SOLVE THE MYSTERY

Color the spaces with a cross: black; with 1 dot: white; with 2 dots: orange; with ▽ brown; with **d:** dark blue; with ——: purple; and with ☽ yellow. When you are done: turn your paper upside down to solve the mystery.

Cut along the dotted lines on the date slips below.

Arrange the slips in order from the earliest date (top of list) to the most recent date (bottom of list). Then glue them in order along the left side of page 2. Make a small drawing or cartoon to the right of each date to go with (to illustrate) that date.

A.D. 1400   Most Plains people become farmers

c. 6,000-1000 B.C.   Most people on the Plains are Hunters-wild plant gatherers

1866   Native American lands are given to the railroad builders.

1869   The railroad across the U.S.A. is finished.

c.1590   All tribes (except Blackfeet in N. & Comanche in S.) are farmers.

1829-1890   Wars go on between the Plains tribes and the U.S. Army.

c.7,500-4,500 B.C. Prehistoric hunters roam the Plains.

1885   The buffalo herds are all gone.

1887   The U.S. Government makes 100 reservations and the Native Americans are moved onto them from their homes on the Plains.

A.D. 1700s Horses come to the Great Plains.

A.D. 1600s   Farming tribes move to new lands everytime the soil gets over-used.

c. A.D. 1350 Tribes begin drifting back to the Plains.

c. A.D. 1250 Lack of rain drives the people off the Plains.

Carefully cut these slips apart!

Glue date slips in this space.

Cartoons go here.

Use crayons to color in the wooden railing of the Earth Lodge. Color the lodge light brown. Do NOT color where it says "Glue." Also color the logs on the entrance hall below.

Carefully cut out the Earth Lodge. Apply glue to the part that says (1) "Glue." Then swing the part to the right, over onto the glued part. Hold in place until glue dries.

Next apply glue to (2). Swing (1) over onto the glued part. Repeat these steps for (3) through (6). When they are dry, apply glue to "Glue last" and bring (7) over and place on top of the glued part. Press in place. Trim any loose edges at the top of the lodge.

Apply an even (light) coat of glue to all of the lodge except the railing. Sprinkle with fine dirt and then shake the excess off carefully.

Cut out the entrance hall along the solid lines. Then fold down along the - - - lines. Put glue on the two corner squares and swing them under the middle square. When your entrance hall is complete, glue it to the entry of your Earth Lodge.

Entrance hall to the Earth Lodge.

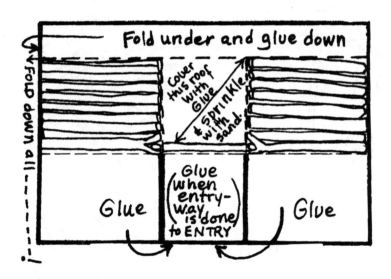

How your completed Earth Lodge will look.

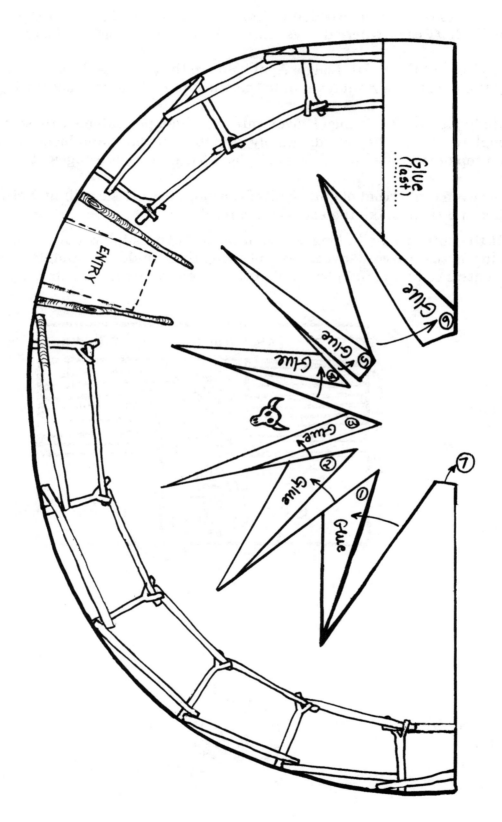

186

Name _____

PLAINS INDIAN FOLLOW-THE-DOTS

Using a pencil, start at 1 and continue on through 151. The picture is from a war shield; you can color it in once you have finished the puzzle.

Name _____

PLAINS TRIBES WORD SEARCH

Look in the puzzle below and try to find the names of 22 Plains Indian tribes.[*] Circle each name as you find it. The names may be written across or down (or backwards). GOOD LUCK!!

B	H	C	E	H	C	A	P	A	I	G	R	O	S
L	I	P	D	T	E	C	A	D	C	R	O	W	V
A	D	W	I	C	H	I	T	A	S	Q	D	K	E
C	S	V	A	E	C	H	E	R	A	U	D	A	N
K	F	E	E	T	N	S	M	A	N	D	A	N	T
O	T	N	A	U	A	I	A	P	A	W	C	B	R
P	A	R	W	Q	M	O	M	A	H	A	R	A	E
O	T	T	O	T	O	U	A	H	P	I	G	R	O
N	N	E	I	E	C	X	N	O	A	S	N	A	K
C	L	A	K	I	O	W	D	A	W	A	P	K	A
A	S	T	A	D	I	H	P	O	N	C	O	I	W
R	I	K	A	E	N	N	E	Y	E	H	C	R	A
D	A	K	O	T	A	P	C	H	E	Q	U	A	P

Here are the 22 tribes to look for:

1. Apache	6. Cheyenne	11. Hidatsa	16. Oto	21. Ute
2. Arapaho	7. Comanche	12. Kansa	17. Pawnee	22. Wichita
3. Arikara	8. Crow	13. Kiowa	18 Ponca	
4. Blackfeet	9. Dakota	14. Mandan	19. Quapaw	
5. Caddo	10. Gros Ventre	15. Omaha	20. Sioux	

[*]or groups

© 1995 by The Center for Applied Research in Education

PLAINS TRIBES WORD SEARCH, ANSWER KEY

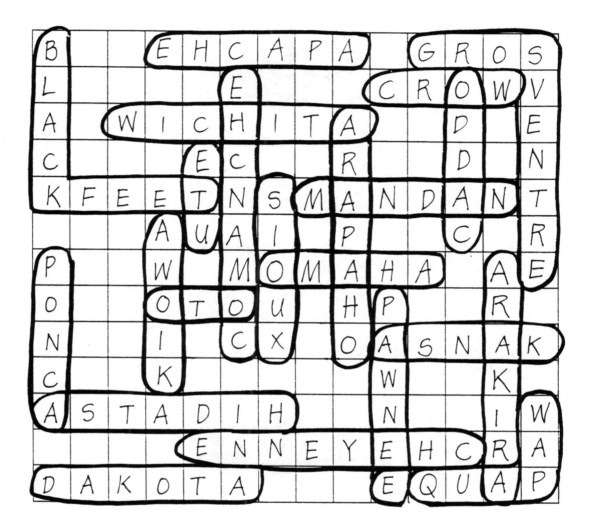

The two groups of people who first lived on the Plains and Prairies were the Hunter Tribes and the Farming Tribes.

Read page 2, which shows the different Times, Food, Shelter, and Trade items of these two groups.

Decide which description in each of these four sections belongs to the Hunter Tribes—and which belongs to the Farming Tribes.

For example: Since the first people on the Plains were the big game HUNTERS . . . their time was . . . (the *earliest* dates given)

Cut out each description on the dotted line and glue it where it belongs on page 3. Good luck!

Cut along the dotted lines to make strips which you will glue in place on page 3.

TIME:

About 7500 B.C. to 4500 B.C.	Prehistoric Hunters on the Plains.
About 4500 B.C. to A.D. 1250	People hunted AND gathered wild plants. Lack of rain drove people off Plains.
About A.D. 1000–1250	Farming villages along the Missouri River up to North Dakota and on the middle Plains.
A.D. 1250–1350	DROUGHT—People left their farms.
About A.D. 1350	People began drifting back to the Plains. Only the Blackfeet (N) and Comanche (S) were nomadic.
About A.D. 1350	Most people who returned to the Plains became farmers.
1700s	Horse came to the Plains: Cheyenne and Sioux became nomadic hunters.
1700s	Horse came to the Plains: Many tribes NOW raised crops AND went on buffalo hunts!
FOOD:	They grew beans, corn, squash, and sunflowers. They harvested wild turnips, milkweed, nuts, and berries.
	They hunted deer, rabbit, buffalo, and elk.
SHELTER:	They lived in portable skin and hide tipis.
	They lived in villages of 70–80 Grass Houses on Plains in the South. They lived in Earth Lodge villages along Missouri and Republic rivers.
TRADE:	They traded their (dried) meat, tipi covers, buffalo robes, hides; the Crow and Sioux traded catlinite pipes, the Cheyenne, Arapaho, and Sioux traded clothing with quillwork on it.
	They traded dried corn, beans, squash, pemmican, nuts, parfleche, and quillwork.

© 1995 by The Center for Applied Research in Education

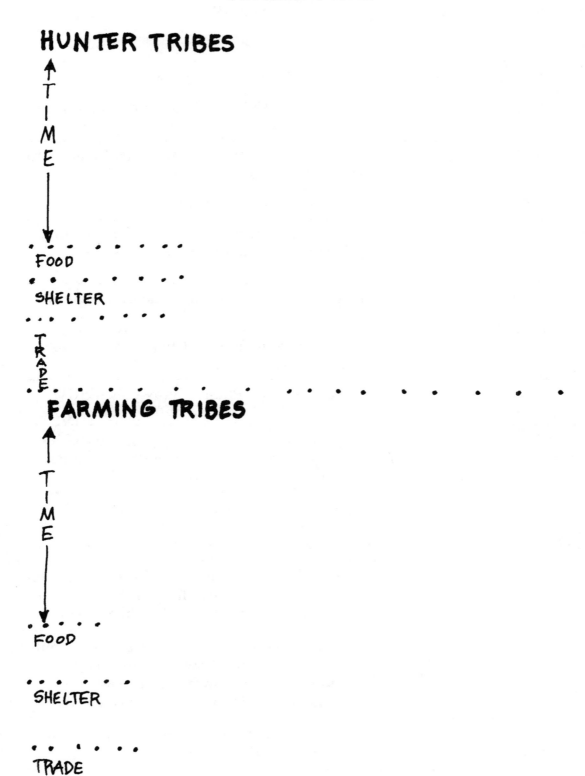

CORNBREAD COOKED ON AN OPEN FIRE

For every 8–10 servings you will need:

a 10″ heavy (cast-iron) skillet
a tight-fitting lid
a hot plate

Each group of 4 students has: a big bowl, measuring cup, a sifter, measuring spoons, a small bowl, big (wooden) spoons and these ingredients:

3 T. bacon drippings (or melted butter)
3/4 cup flour
3 teaspoons baking powder
2 T. sugar (or honey)
3/4 teaspoon salt
3/4 cup cornmeal
1 egg
3 T. melted butter
3/4 cup milk
(toothpicks)

Oil the skillet with the bacon drippings (or butter).
Sift the next 4 ingredients into the big bowl. Add the cornmeal to the bowl. (Turn hot plate on to LOW.)

Break the egg into the small bowl. Beat the egg. Add the last 2 ingredients to the egg. Beat this well. Pour the egg mixture into the cornmeal mixture. Mix them up with *just 5 or 6 quick stirs.*

Pour the batter into the oiled skillet. Cover with the lid. Place skillet on hot plate (turned to LOW). Cook for 1/2 hour. Remove lid. Test to see if cornbread is done by sticking a toothpick in the middle & pulling it out. If the toothpick is sticky cover skillet & cook some more. If it comes out clean your cornbread is DONE! Eat it with honey—just like the Prairie & Plains people did!

THE PLAINS INDIANS

Teacher's Resource Guide

TEACHER'S RESOURCE GUIDE

TEACHING MANUALS

In Search of Our Past

This U.S. History teaching manual includes a unit on Native American women, giving a story, plus background information.

Distributed by Education Development Center, 55 Chapel Street, Newton, MA 02160

Teaching About Native Americans by Harvey Harjo

Bulletin #8
National Council for the Social Studies, 3501 Newark Street NW, Washington, D.C. 20016-3167

BIBLIOGRAPHY

Through Indian Eyes—Books Without Bias by Beverly Slapin and Doris Seale (Berkeley, CA: Oyate Press, 2702 Mathews Street, 94702)

MAP

Ethnological Map #02816

38" × 32" ($7.95 + $4.75 S&H)
National Geographic Society, P.O. Box 96094, Washington D.C. 20077-9191. Request current price list.

BOOKS

Women in American Indian Society by Reyna Green (Chelsea House Publishers)

For children in grades 3-6, this is part of the series *Indians of North America* which includes many titles, among them several about specific tribes such as the Arapaho, Choctaw, and Comanche.

197

I Am the Fire of Time: Voices of Native American Women, Jane B. Katz, editor (E. P. Dutton, Publishers)

The short accounts will interest older students.

Re-thinking Columbus Day	$ 4
State of Native Americans	$16
Thinking and Re-thinking U.S. History	$21

Request book list from CED (Center for Establishing Dialogue in Teaching), 325 E. Southern Avenue, Suite #107, Tempe, AZ 85282; (602) 894-1333.

Buffalo Bird Woman's Garden as told to Gilbert L. Wilson (1987, a reprint of the 1917 publication)

The Way to Independence, Memories of a Hidatsa Indian Family, 1840–1920 by Carolyn Gilman and Mary Jane Schneider (1987)

An outstanding compendium of photos and narrative.

Both of the two above books are published by The Minnesota Historical Society Press, St. Paul, MN 55101.

White Buffalo's Story: The Story of Montana's Indians

Oral history with a very easy-going tone. Meaty, 65 pages, low vocabulary. Ask for the catalog (*many* good titles are available): Montana Council for Indian Education, P.O. 31215, Billings, MT 59107.

The Cheyenne by Arthur Myers (1992, Franklin Watts Company) ($6)

Excellent illustrations, clear straight-forward text. Also in this series:
The Shoshoni by Alden R. Carter
The Sioux by Elaine Landau

Native Americans, a New True Book by Jay Miller (1993, Children's Press) ($5)

Indian Signals and Sign Language by George Fronval and Daniel Dubois (Bonanza Books, Crown Publishers)

An excellent reference book with many clear photos to illustrate the signs.

North American Indian Arts by Andrew Hunter Whiteford (Golden Press, Western Publishing Co.).

Small in size, but huge in value: $5; a Golden Guide book

Native American Architecture by Peter Nabokov and Robert Easton (Oxford University Press)

The definitive book on this subject, and much more.

MAGAZINES

Skipping Stones, a Multi-cultural Children's Quarterly

vol. 4, No. 4, *Indigenous Societies* / Rain forest
vol. 4, No. 3, *Focus on Native Societies of the Americas*
A wealth of addresses, activities, interviews.
To order: P.O. Box 3939, Eugene OR 97403-0939; (503) 342-4956.

Cobblestone: The History Magazine for Young Children

July 1982, *America's Cowboys*
August 1981, *The Story of America's Buffalo*
Rich variety of information, addresses, illustrations. ($5.70 each back issue, $23 for yearly subscription)
Order from: Cobblestone, 7 School Street, Peterborough, NH 03458; (603) 924-7209.

TAPES: SONGS, LEGENDS, DRUMMING

Indian Sounds: Favorite American Indian Music Tapes

Write and ask for the price list ($15 for the first tape, $12 for each additional) from National Native American Co-op, San Carlos, AZ 85550-1000.

A selection of Native American tapes is also available from:

Indian House, Box 472, Taos, NM 87571; (505) 776-2953.

POSTER AND COLORING BOOK

Harmony • The Seasons • The Sun • The Soil • The Water

Poster is bright, colorful, inspirational. The company also offers a copy of the *Living in Harmony Coloring Book*. (See below)
Order from: Soil Conservation Service, Public Information Division, P.O. 2890, Washington, D.C., 20013; 1-800-THE SOIL.

Living in Harmony Coloring Book

Simple line drawings teach conservation. Developed on Flathead Reservation, Montana. Has text in English and Kootenai.
$1.35 for single copy, or $ .57 @ + shipping for large quantities; from National Association of Conservation Districts, 408 E. Main, P.O. 855, League City, TX 77573; 1-800-825-5547.

PLEASE NOTE: All prices are subject to change without notice.

▷ NOTES ◁

≫ NOTES ≪

▶ NOTES ◀